The Bo

Gabrielle Morris, 24, is an English graduate from London University. Her slender acting talents, she says, amount to making a crisis out of a drama. Until compiling The Book of Luvvies, she thought a prima donna was a large kebab. Her writing has appeared in the Guardian, the Sunday Times, the Mail on Sunday and the Yorkshire Post. She lives in Preston and reports on women's issues for the Lancashire Evening Post.

Jonathan Margolis's acting debut was as King Theseus in an Essex production of A Midsummer Night's Dream. It was suggested after the 2-night run that he might make a journalist. He now writes for the Sunday Times among other publications, and was John Cleese's unofficial biographer.

Also by Gabrielle Morris and Jonathan Margolis

THE COMMUTER'S TALE

The Book of Luvvies

GABRIELLE MORRIS
And
JONATHAN MARGOLIS

CHAPMANS

Chapmans Publishers
A division of the Orion Publishing Group Ltd
Orion House
5 Upper St Martin's Lane
London WC2H 9EA

A CIP catalogue record for this book is available
from the British Library
ISBN 1 85592 655 5

First published by Chapmans 1993

Typeset by Deltatype Ltd, Ellesmere Port,
Cheshire
Printed by Clays Ltd, St Ives plc

For darling Ken and Em. And also
Josh and Sue.

Preface

When we decided to compile a book of funny, ridiculous, embarrassing and downright incredible stories about actors and performers, we were determined to do two things to make the collection different from the usual actors' after-dinner reminiscences.

Firstly, we would search widely for our anecdotes – we wanted to include stories about the rich and famous, the household names, but we were convinced that some of the best tales would inevitably come from amateur dramatic groups, long-forgotten professional shows in provincial towns and even from fringe arts like morris dancing (well, we said this was just a first idea!) and obscure sources abroad. The second part of the plan was that we would only allow stories that made us laugh. The problem with most actors' tales, as told on ten million TV chat shows, is that they aren't funny unless you happen to be an actor and, preferably, know all the people involved personally. Actors tend to relate such anecdotes to show how many other actors they know, and what absolute darlings they all are to work with, rather than with any idea of entertaining the non-luvvie. The really daft stories are usually swept under the carpet, which is from where, by and large, we have attempted to retrieve them.

We hope you enjoy them. And by the way — don't imagine for a moment that when we refer to luvvies, we don't like them as a profession. Far from it. We have found them absolute darlings . . . especially to write about.

1
It'll Be All Wrong on the Night

The Welsh actors Ruth and Philip Madoc were in a provincial stage production of the radio play *Under Milk Wood*. They had just got to the 'Bible black' bit everyone loves when a loud voice was heard from the wings. 'Who order these-a sanga-wiches?' it demanded. Then, even more insistently, 'I say, WHO ORDER THESE-A SANGA-WICHES?' A waiter from a nearby hotel, it turned out, had come across the road to the theatre to deliver a tray of food. Philip Madoc, sitting dramatically in a single spotlight, rescued the situation with panache. 'Ladies and gentlemen,' he said, 'I think we'd better start again.'

*　　*　　*

Petula Clark held the audience spellbound as she played her death-bed scene; some tears were even beginning to flow among the emotional theatregoers. Suddenly, as if somehow it knew what was expected of it, the bed promptly collapsed. The mood was ruined as the audience dissolved into fits of laughter.

*　　*　　*

One of Peter O'Toole's first roles was as a Georgian peasant in a Chekhov play. His part was to come on stage and say, 'Dr Ostroff, the horses are ready.' O'Toole was determined to make the best of the role, and practised it endlessly, interpreting it in various ways. On the first night, his concentration at fever pitch, he came on and announced gravely, 'Dr Horsey, the ostroffs are ready.'

*　　*　　*

Neil Baines was playing a Chinese policeman in the panto *Aladdin* at the Tameside Theatre outside Manchester. As part of the show, Neil was to be blown out of a car by a fake explosion. Clearly a pupil of the Method School, he fell so realistically, he managed to knock himself out. Whilst he was being removed from the stage the rest of the cast tried to ad lib. They were so successful that soon the audience were roaring with laughter, and failed to realise anything was amiss.

A grandmother got an unexpected piece of the action when she and her daughter went to see a production of *Hamlet* at the Pittsburgh Three Rivers Shakespeare Festival. Sitting in the third row of the stalls, Patricia Sapphic was struck by a dagger which slipped from actor Richard McMillan's hands during a stage fight. The long-bladed knife flew across the stage and struck Mrs Sapphic right between the eyes. Hamlet, temporarily forgetting his own 'To be or not to be' dilemma, jumped into the audience to help try to stop the flow of blood that was gushing from the injured woman's forehead. Mrs Sapphic's daughter Mary Beth turned to Hamlet and demanded, 'Why don't you use rubber props, for God's sake?' Hamlet could do nothing but apologise profusely. Mrs Sapphic was taken to hospital where the dagger was removed and the wound stitched up. Later at home she said, 'I'm sure Shakespeare didn't have this in mind when he wrote it!'

*   *   *

A travelling stage magician became the talk of the

town in Takoradi, West Ghana. His unique act involved shooting his assistant and then bringing him back to life. However, in this particular display, he had to report what he insisted was his first failure. The unfortunate assistant failed to revive, despite 30 minutes of incantations. The magician informed the police that he had performed the feat many times before with the same assistant.

* * *

In a Bangor hospital, doctors rushed to attend to the man who was wheeled in with his throat spectacularly slit. But then Steve O'Hara sat up and announced, 'Hang on, I'm only acting.' Steve then explained that the blood was make-up for his part as a murder victim — he'd come to have a dodgy ankle seen to … he'd hurt it whilst on stage.

* * *

Two whole minutes into his act at Ripon Race-course in North Yorkshire, escapologist Geoff Brownhut suddenly realised that the overzealous volunteers from the audience had shackled him too tightly — and he was chained up with a high-velocity crossbow primed to fire at him at close range. Hidden from the audience by a curtain and a piece of board, Geoff had no choice but to sit tight and hold his breath. Travelling at 300 feet per second, the arrow zoomed straight through the curtain and the board, missing his head by just 2 inches. The 300 guests only realised what had gone wrong when they saw that Geoff was still bound up.

* * *

It was the dramatic climax of a play in a Glasgow theatre. The expensive revolving set (can't you smell trouble coming?) was supposed to change from a ballroom into a prison cell by one simple revolution of the stage. No problem ... until the stage discovered that it enjoyed spinning round and round. It carried on merrily turning from ballroom to jail and back again 33 times, while the actors clung on to the props for dear life and the audience (surprise surprise) dissolved into laughter.

* * *

The wicked squire in the pantomime *Mother Goose* got more than he'd bargained for when a live goose got into her part with gusto and attacked him. Gertie the goose, who had been borrowed from a neighbouring farm in Rotherham, South Yorkshire, took an instant dislike to actor Roger Staniforth who was playing wicked Squire Hardup, and began hissing and squawking at him. Unfortunately, at that very moment the poor squire was involved in a sword fight with the principal boy and, in stepping aside to avoid the big bird, ended up on the point of his adversary's sword. Principal boy Les Kendrick recalled, 'We were in the middle of a sword fight when suddenly the goose came tearing across at Roger. The next thing I knew, my sword was sticking in his side.' Meanwhile the squire, after returning from the hospital where he'd had his wounds stitched, refused to be frightened by Gertie. He stated resolutely, 'The show must go on whether the goose likes me or not.'

*　　　*　　　*

Ian McKellen as Romeo once made an unscripted hasty exit from Juliet's bedroom. Stepping over the side of her balcony and putting his foot on to the rope ladder, the unfortunate lover fell 15 feet through the air and landed on the floor when a wooden rung gave way. Luckily McKellen was not hurt and managed to continue as though nothing had happened. At the end of the play however, when taking his curtain call, McKellen was holding the offending rung.

* * *

Toyah Willcox was taking part in the *Taming Of The Shrew*. In the fight scene in Act One, Toyah's fellow actress was obviously deeply engrossed in her role, and dished out more than was necessary. She head-butted Toyah, leaving her with a broken jaw. But Toyah carried on for two hours until the performance was over before letting a doctor wire her jaw.

* * *

Meanwhile in Rotherham, comic Bobby King, playing the part of Nurse Glucose, was being hit over the head with a plastic bottle. One fellow actor proved a tad over-enthusiastic, and Bobby ended up unconscious in hospital. His next difficulty was explaining to the nurses why he was wearing a nightgown and scarlet knickers.

* * *

The opera I *Pagliacci* was livened up by an un-scheduled choreographic flourish when the tenor came on stage. As usual, he stepped from behind a closed curtain to commence the Prologue, but as luck would have it, this night the curtain was in line with the orchestra pit. The hapless tenor stepped into thin air. Making a desperate grab for the curtain to stop himself from falling into the pit, the tenor managed to swing himself back on to the stage, where he proceeded to open the opera in the more customary and dignified manner.

*　　*　　*

During filming of *The Snows of Kilimanjaro*, actor Gregory Peck had to carry his co-star Ava Gardner across the set. This display of chivalry had its down-side when he slipped and tore several ligaments in his leg. He finished up in plaster.

*　　*　　*

Actor Hugh Griffith's starring role in *The Caucasian Chalk Circle* was nearly his last – he almost killed himself. Griffith explained, 'One night I was doing the hanging scene – the one where the soldiers are trying to frighten me – when I slipped off the box.' This would have been okay, if only he had not already been wearing the noose round his neck at the time. 'The next thing I remember was being brought round with brandy and smelling-salts in the wings,' recounts Griffith.

*　　*　　*

Shakespeare's plays, with their fights and general on-stage boisterousness, can be bad for actors' health at the best of times. In the case of *Macbeth* (a play most actors superstitiously refuse even to name) thespians find themselves truly in the danger zone. A typical case in point was during a production of *Macbeth* at Chesterfield's Civic Theatre. Towards the end of the play the authentic sound of clashing swords was accompanied by an even more impressive spurt of blood. Macbeth, played by Brian Rawlinson, looked at his hand, saw a deep gash and collapsed. Earlier in the week, other members of the cast had fared just as badly: Banquo, played by Ronald Harwood, had been knocked unconscious, and another unfortunate had fallen through the trap-door.

*   *   *

In 1956, the cast of West End company The Silver Whistle were informed that the Queen Mother and her entourage would be coming to see their show. The theatre management hurriedly ordered champagne for the royal box, decked the theatre out in flowers and had everyone down to the backstage cat wearing their best clothes for the great event. Too bad that the call from Clarence House was a hoax.

*   *   *

Audrey Hepburn suffered from being battered about during the filming of *My Fair Lady*. In her part as the Cockney flower girl, Eliza Doolittle, the delicate actress had to be knocked across the set in torrential rain. Unfortunately, the sequence didn't go according to plan and had to be reshot. Then the reshoot wasn't satisfactory, nor was the third take. In fact, that particular scene had to be repeated several dozen times before the director was happy. By this time Hepburn was wearing cricket pads beneath her old-fashioned bloomers to prevent serious damage.

*　　*　　*

The American opera star Shirley Verrett had to beat a huge gong with a mallet during one performance at Covent Garden. She did so with such enthusiasm that the mallet head shot off and flew across the stage. It lay there until it was stuck back together by a stagehand. In the meantime, Miss Verrett had to mime beating the gong with just the headless stick.

*　　*　　*

At one classic performance of the opera *Rigoletto*, the baritone playing the hunchback was surprised to hear laughter during what should have been an emotional and moving scene. Looking behind him, he saw that his hump had slipped down, turning him from a deformed pity-inspiring character to a figure of fun with an oversize bottom. Managing to finish the scene, the singer sped tearfully off the stage amidst roars of laughter from the audience.

* * *

An Italian tenor sneaked out of a production of *Carmen* to have a swift drink in a nearby bar. It was there that he drew the attention of a policeman who, on seeing the singer's ripped army uniform, thought he was a deserter and promptly arrested him. After spending some minutes protesting his innocence, the tenor realised that there was only one thing left to do: he broke into song and serenaded the officers for a minute or two, they applauded the impromptu performance, then escorted him back to the theatre.

* * *

Abraham Mulder spent six years perfecting his act, the *pièce de résistance* of which was to set fire to himself and then dive into water to put himself out again. A theatrical agent from Johannesburg hinted that he might take Mulder on if he managed to get some publicity. Mulder achieved the publicity, but sadly not for the right reason. The 49-year-old invited members of the press to come and watch him perform by a dam. When all the media had gathered, Mulder stood on a ladder above the dam and doused himself liberally with petrol. One reporter kindly pointed out that the ladder didn't look at all safe but Mulder ignored him. He duly struck a match just as the ladder collapsed, and fell gloriously aflame on to the grass below. Yelling, he leapt into the reservoir. But it wasn't over yet – as he emerged from the water the smouldering grass re-lit the residue of petrol left on his clothes and he had to dive back into the water. Later and rather subdued, Mulder excused himself by saying he had been put off by the photographers. 'I suppose if no agent will give me a chance, I'll just have to continue doing this to amuse my friends,' he said.

*　　*　　*

Nineteen-year-old Bryan Evans landed the prestigious part of the gorilla in the musical *Hair*, but the role turned out to be even hairier than he expected. One evening, just before curtain up, he got stuck in the lift. While other members of the cast began to panic because he was wearing the only gorilla suit the company possessed, the unfortunate Bryan was desperately shouting for help. Luckily an electrician heard him calling and 10 minutes later, Bryan was free, just in time to swing into the performance.

*　　*　　*

An actress on stage in the West End had to hurl a plate to the floor in a fit of fury. It is not hard to imagine her astonishment when the plate bounced back.

*　　*　　*

Actor David Beale nearly lost his head during a performance of A Man For All Seasons. Beale had taken the title role of Sir Thomas More, which culminates in his execution in the final scene. Laying his head on the block, as he had done many times before, David got ready to pull the secret lever which would simultaneously retract the block with his head on it and release a dummy head which would tumble on to the stage. But to the actor's horror, the lever didn't operate properly and Dave was left facing the axe. The executioner, Donald Cotton, not realising that anything was amiss, swung his axe down fairly and squarely on Dave's neck. The block was covered in blood and Dave needed 6 stiches in his wound. As a member of the cast pointed out, it was only the fact that it was a wooden axe that had prevented a terrible accident. The following night, Dave was back on stage with a huge headache. He commented, 'I can't imagine that people who were beheaded knew much about it.'

*　　*　　*

Jack was already 20 feet up his beanstalk before he realised there was a problem. Jack, played by 27-year-old singer Paul Rhodes, found out that his beanstalk, a metal frame, was not as solid as it looked when the contraption collapsed under his weight during rehearsals. Falling 20 feet on to the concrete floor, Paul hit the property mistress Jo Jackson while the beanstalk crashed to the floor in bits, setting off a fire-alarm sprinkler which flooded the orchestra pit. Later, tucked up in his hospital bed, Paul explained, 'When I turned to wave to the audience from the beanstalk, it gave way. I hit the trap-door which is disguised as a well and landed heavily on the floor. It was quite chaotic. And I always thought it was the giant who fell – not Jack!' Paul's accident meant that he missed the entire five-week run of the panto.

*　　*　　*

Actor Maynard Williams was playing the part of a

roller-skating train in the West End hit musical *Starlight Express*. One night, Maynard made his entrance by skating on to the stage – and then made an immediate exit by falling off into the auditorium. Unlike the more conventional type of train, he did however manage to continue with his performance.

*   *   *

When part of the ceiling fell on to the stage during a performance, the comedian Roy Kinnear raced on stage and kept the audience calm by cracking a few jokes. Roy was starring alongside Charlton Heston in *A Man For All Seasons* when the decorative masonry from the balcony decided to make its stage debut. Whilst staff sealed off the area, Roy reassured the audience, 'They really knew how to build theatres in those days,' despite all the evidence to the contrary.

*   *   *

In 1910 a play at the old Paragon Theatre in London contained a scene in which a sea-faring vessel had to lurch through stormy seas. To achieve this ambitious effect, a massive tank was installed on the stage with machinery to make the water ripple. Naturally, one night the machinery failed and the theatre firemen were called in to make waves by using their pumps. But all was to go terribly wrong. One of the pumps went awry, drenching the orchestra and the audience in the stalls with thousands of gallons of high-pressure water.

*   *   *

Ann Crumb, starring in the musical *Aspects of Love* alongside Michael Ball, had a slight mishap in front of hundreds of theatregoers when her foot got trapped in the revolving stage. It happened just after the scene in which Ann's stage husband dies and, as she embraces another character, darkness descends on the stage. But as Ann turned to leave she remembers, 'All of a sudden, I felt my foot being grabbed and pulled. I guess I put my other foot out to counteract it, but then that went in too.' Realising that she was trapped, Ann started screaming with pain. Luckily her cries were heard by the stage crew, and the machinery was switched off. Fellow actor Tim Nilsson-Page scooped her up and carried her to her dressing-room. Ann had to spend nine days in hospital and undergo an operation on her foot.

*   *   *

The realistic sword fights in *Treasure Island* delighted the audience at a theatre in Oldham, Lancashire. Unfortunately for the cast, the injuries were all too real. In the first week of the production, the theatre ran out of plasters and bandages due to wounds inflicted on stage. In the second week, John Cooper, playing Captain Smollett, had to be rushed to hospital with a cartilage injury; he made his entrance the following night with the aid of a walking stick. Black Dog, played by Richard Frost, cracked his head on a beam and had to have stiches; he came on stage the next night with his head swathed in bandages. Then Israel Hands, played by Michael Haynes, fell and injured his back. Even Carl Paulsen the director managed to sustain an injury. He vowed that he would never do the play again, adding, 'I have never been so glad to see the end of a play.'

* * *

In New Dehli in 1966, a human cannonball's career reached an explosive climax when two circus hands fired the cannon too early. Shankar Prasad was blown to smithereens.

* * *

Strongman Walter Cornelius was a bit cut up after

appearing on BBC TV's *Blue Peter*. Walter, a 15-stone Latvian, was performing his party trick which consisted of smashing a paving-stone on his head with a sledge hammer. A splinter of stone left the strongman with a cut that needed two stitches. He commented later, 'I have been doing this act in circuses all over the world for 18 years, and I have never been hurt before.'

*   *   *

In Nantes, France, scantily-clad opera singer Rita Capri delighted audiences by reaching top E in her final chorus . . . and then delighted them some more when her knickers fell down. Her partner picked them up and Rita, not missing a note, flung them into the wings.

*   *   *

Henry Warren had spent 41 years walking on broken glass, bending bars of iron and lying on beds of nails. So he was unperturbed when he started to perform his famous strangulation act in front of the big crowd which had gathered at Tower Hill in London. Henry would invite six big men to have a tug of war on a chain which was wrapped round his neck. (The chain never failed to break before his neck did.) On this occasion, however, there was only one man pulling on each end of the chain when Henry suddenly collapsed, striking his eye on the cobbles as he fell. When he woke up in hospital, he was so ashamed that he discharged himself against advice and went home. Later he mused, 'It is the first time my act has failed.'

*　　*　　*

A production of *Calamity Jane* nearly ended in disaster when the theatre staff were sold live bullets instead of fake ones. The gunsmith alerted the police as soon as he discovered his mistake, and officers traced them to the Palace Theatre at Watford only hours before an actor was due to fire them as part of the show.

*　　*　　*

Opera stars had to give their performances by climbing up ladders when the safety curtain stuck during a production of *Le Nozze di Figaro* at Covent Garden. In between the second and third acts, the curtain had been lowered as required by law, but when stage hands tried to raise it again, the thing would not budge. In a sparkling display of pragmatism, it was decided that the lead singers would perform in front of the curtain whilst the chorus would be placed in the orchestra pit. Ladders were strategically sited so that the nine soloists, including Sir Geraint Evans, could clamber from the pit and into position. Having hastily organised all this, the backstage staff were almost disappointed when, without warning and bang on time, the safety curtain went up of its own accord. The show went on after only a brief delay.

*   *   *

The opera singer Lauritz Melchior was in the final act of a production of *Lohengrin*, where he had to saunter on to a magnificent swan-shaped boat to sail serenely away into the wings. As disaster cognoscenti have come to expect, one night the boat sailed off before Melchior had managed to get into it. Without batting an eyelid the singer turned to the audience and enquired, 'What time does the next swan go?'

*   *   *

It was a missing chariot that caused even more confusion during an English National Opera production of *The Magic Flute*. Keith Erwen as Tamino and Niall Murray as Papageno waited patiently for their chariot, which would sup- posedly be ridden by three spirit boys. Neither chariot nor spirits materialised. Papageno hinted subtly, 'I think I can hear a chariot coming.' 'Yes,' agreed Tamino, 'so can I.' Then he turned to the audience and said, 'No wonder it's late. That chariot runs on standard British Rail gauge, you know.' The audience were delighted but the technical administrator was less than pleased. He spent the entire following morning riding up and down in the chariot, trying to find out what was wrong with it.

*   *   *

Paul Newman was so embarrassed about his first movie that he took out a newspaper advertisement to apologise to the public. The star's debut had been in *The Silver Chalice* which had won the distinguished title of 'The Worst Movie Of The Fifties'.

*   *   *

Robin Askwith, the star of the film *Confessions Of A Window Cleaner*, admitted to a court that there were off-stage hazards to being a ladykiller. Robin was giving evidence at a court in Southend, Essex on behalf of his chauffeur, one Mr Small, who was on trial for speeding. Robin explained that he and his producer had attended a reception in Southend for his latest film, and on leaving had been threatened by a gang of youths. Robin claimed: 'They shouted, "We know who you are." They were threatening and I thought I would be attacked.' He then proceeded to explain how his chauffeur had hurried them both into the car and had driven off at speed. Robin continued: 'On the way back to London, we became aware of bright headlights behind us. I said to him, "I hope it's not those thugs." Mr Small tried to get rid of them and accelerated in case we were in danger.' It transpired that the headlights were not being shone by jealous yobbos, but by a police car. Giving weight to his plea of fear, Robin told the court of the occasion that a window cleaner had knocked him down in a pub on the grounds that the star's best-known film had given the window-cleaning profession a bad name. Meanwhile Mr Small, a chauffeur of 12 years' standing, admitted that he had to put his foot down on previous occasions in order to avoid trouble. He was fined and had his licence endorsed. Leaving the court, Robin admitted: 'In my films, I'm lucky with the ladies. Some people seem to resent this and say "What have you got that I haven't?"'

*   *   *

About the turn of the century, Eugene Sandow

offered a novelty act with a difference. He was a strongman who could undertake any display of strength without disturbing the fig leaf which covered his private parts!

*   *   *

A novelty act which enjoyed top billing in Australia was performed by one Paul Cinquevalli, whose amazing feat was to play billiards on his back. Paul arrived at one venue to be told that the crowd was so keen to see him that he was the star of the evening, and was the sole act for the second half of the show. This left Paul with a problem – his act only lasted a total of eight minutes.

*   *   *

Deptford nightclub impresario Malcolm Hardee had once been part of a novelty act called 'The Greatest Show On Legs'. It consisted of three naked men passing balloons to one another without revealing their private parts. Hardee then went on to encourage other novelty acts and produced a TV pilot show called *Hardee's Half Hour*. Explaining the process of choosing only the best novelty acts for his show, Hardee explained that he had rejected one performer called 'Karen and Her Amazing Dogs' on the grounds that 'She only had one dog and it wasn't that amazing.' Likewise, the man who blew bubbles out of his ears because, as Hardee explained, 'It sounds good but it was bloody boring.' Instead, he chose a housewife from Chelmsford who inserted her fingers into her mouth and whistled 'Lara's Theme' and the music from *Gone With The Wind*. Other favoured acts were provided by septuagenarian Rex Roper, a cowboy lassooist, and his sidekick Norman who wore an army jacket and helmet with suspender belt and fishnet stockings. The climax of this duo's act was to give a rendition of 'Brother Can You Spare A Dime'. Hardee added tentatively, 'I think it was an anti-war statement.'

*   *   *

Dave Flame's novelty act involved asking a member of the audience to smash a concrete slab on his chest with a sledgehammer, but he should have known better than to allow a cross-eyed man to volunteer. As a result Dave suffered a broken sternum.

*   *   *

An actor at the Queen's Theatre in Manchester was supposed to declaim, 'Stand back, my lord and let the coffin pass,' but what came out was,

'Stand back, my lord and let the parson cough.' Similarly, an actor in one New York theatre turned the exclamation, 'Royal bold Caesar,' into that delicious dish, 'Boiled rolled Caesar!'

* * *

A play called *The Fire Worshippers* was being performed at a Surrey Theatre, and in one scene an actor had to ride across the stage on a live camel. In the middle of the stage a trap-door gave way under the camel's weight and the animal fell part-way through, breaking its neck. The actor leapt off unhurt and the play continued as best it could with all the main action taking place around the dead beast's head.

* * *

Actor John Kemble was seriously disturbed on stage one night by a crying child in the audience. Finally, unable to bear it any longer, he turned to the audience and said, 'Ladies and Gentlemen, unless the play is stopped the child cannot possibly go on.'

* * *

A small touring theatre company once performed

in a Yorkshire village to an audience of two. On seeing the men sitting there, the stage manager went on to explain that, since there was a shortage of theatregoers, the play would not be performed, but the two men could have their money refunded. The men steadfastly refused to take their money and leave . . . they turned out to be bailiffs who'd come to repossess some of the company's props.

* * *

In 1954, a 17-year-old would-be actor had been hanging around outside the National Theatre in Washington in the hope of finding some work. Work he did find, but not quite what he had in mind. The play that was about to open was being threatened by a sudden invasion of rats, and the acting union Equity, concerned about the safety of the actors, pressed the theatre management to hire a professional rat-catcher . . . the job went to one Warren Beatty.

2
Such a Darling To Work With

Acting has been described as the only profession where you meet someone for the first time at 8 o'clock in the morning and before lunch have your tongue down their throat. Some stage kisses, however, are more fun than others. Diana Rigg, staring opposite George Lazenby in *On Her Majesty's Secret Service*, disliked him so much that she ate garlic before their love scenes. In the raunchy movie *Nine and a Half Weeks*, one would be forgiven for assuming that Kim Basinger and Mickey Rourke got on like a house on fire. But apparently, despite the erotic scenes where the couple go through the entire contents of a fridge, they couldn't stand one another. The producer of the film, Anthony Isaacs, admitted that the two stars would not even get in the same lift together;

Basinger alleged that kissing Rourke was like 'kissing an ashtray'!

*   *   *

Colin Firth had a down-to-earth attitude when it came to stage romance. In the film *Valmont*, an entire day was spent shooting one long kiss between Firth and his leading lady Meg Tilly. The director, insisting it should be perfect, shot the same intimate scene on three different lenses and in three different states of undress. Firth said, 'The main thing was I had to carry her round the room over and over again. In the end it's workaday. You've just had a bacon sandwich and they can see your spots.'

*   *   *

Tom Cruise got to perform a sizzling love scene in the film *All the Right Moves* with Lea Thompson. Yet Cruise admitted that this was only his second love scene and he still found it odd to take his clothes off with someone who was a virtual stranger . . . so both stars completed the scene with their socks on!

*   *   *

Neither was the film *An Officer and a Gentleman* quite as romantic as it appeared. Female lead Debra Winger revealed that performing opposite Richard Gere was not that wonderful. Debra said, 'What people see as pure passion was really pure misery. On the cutting-room floor there were shots of me in tears. I've never felt less for a co-star than I did for Gere. The last thing I did was think sexy – I save that for home.

*　　*　　*

Even church bell-ringing is a type of performing art ... and bell-ringers such as Mr Ralph Bickers of Lowestoft, Suffolk go to any lengths to be stout troupers, Mr Bickers, 59, realised after over two hours of ringing that he was losing his trousers. This was unusually embarrassing because with him in the belfry was the person in whose honour the special peal (of bells, that is) was taking place. Miss Anne Corney was due to be presented with the Queen's Guide Badge. Mr Bickers struggled for 15 minutes to stop his trousers from falling round his ankles. Valiantly he grasped them with one hand and somehow managed to pull the heavy bellrope with the other. In the end, the tussle became too much and our hero decided to stop ringing. He explained, 'There was a lady present. Anyway, my trousers didn't fall down –

they just slipped to a dangerous level.' He added that he had been called out in a hurry and had forgotten his braces.

*　　　*　　　*

Actor Gavin Abbott performed an even more spectacular feat of trouperdom (although not one that Equity might be too keen on) by taking roles in two plays which were showing at the same time. Gavin, 22, had to play the role of Nym in Shakespeare's *The Merry Wives Of Windsor* at the Bristol New Vic. After the second act, he would divest himself of doublet and hose and don a dinner jacket to race down the road to the Theatre Royal, where he was in Alan Bennett's *Habeas Corpus*. He then had to make it back to the New Vic in time for the curtain call. Gavin admitted, 'It's panicky. Sometimes I get as little as five minutes to change roles, clothes and theatres.'

*　　　*　　　*

In the same city, in 1988, Tim Perrin managed to pull off the same theatrical coup. Tim had the leading role in *Stags and Hens* at Bristol's Old Vic Studio when he landed the part of Mae West's boyfriend, Big Boy in *Happy as a Sandbag* at the Theatre Royal. The 6 foot 6 inch tall ex-policeman's solution was to accept both roles and race the 500 yards between theatres. Charging out of *Happy as a Sandbag*, Tim had 15 minutes to make it to the set of *Stags and Hens*, change and be on time for his cue. Tim promised, 'This one will run and run.'

* * *

Actor Peter Peverley had a heavy role when he appeared in a play in Newcastle. At every performance he had to wade through a liver hotpot, three bags of chips, four sandwiches and a bowl of jelly.

* * *

The female star of *Dirty Dancing*, Jennifer Grey, had the enviable task of performing a love scene with heart-throb Patrick Swayze. Yet Jennifer was apparently so perturbed about flashing her boobs on screen that she put tape over them.

* * *

Verdi's opera *Il Trovatore* was playing in Dublin with star billing to a diva noted for her perfectionism. When the tenor made his entrance a split second too late, she hurled him across the stage and broke his arm whilst singing at the top of her voice, 'No, no, it cannot be.'

* * *

Tallulah Bankhead once bragged that she could upstage another actress without even coming on stage. To demonstrate this, she chose a scene where her opposite number was engaged in a long phone call, and she had to put down her champagne glass and exit. One evening, she placed the glass down so precariously, half on and half off the table, that the audience ignored the actress on the phone to stare in fascination at the glass. Tallulah had, it turned out, put double-sided sticky tape on the bottom of the glass to pull the trick off.

* * *

In such awe was Sarah Bernhardt held that one callboy in Paris would inform her of her call by saying, 'It will be 8.30 when it suits you, Miss Bernhardt.

* * *

Nickolas Grace was in a performance of *The Comedy Of Errors* which lived up to its title.

Nickolas's role consisted of performing a series of acrobatics, cartwheels, and generally leaping around. At the end of the play he would round the audience shaking hands. One evening a gentleman on the front row grabbed Nickolas's hand to congratulate him on a wonderful performance, and as the actor turned to go the gentleman, by way of an encore, thumped him enthusiastically on the back of the leg. Nickolas felt a sharp pain and barely managed to make it back to the wings where he rolled around in agony. The doctor later told him that he had snapped a tendon and would have to have an operation. Nickolas was advised that he would be out of action for three months, but he was finally allowed back on to the stage on condition that he used a crutch.

*   *   *

Actor Bob Mason had to be hit over the head with a chair as part of a saloon brawl during a Wild West play in Rochdale, the wild north-west. Although the chair was made out of a plastic foam which disintegrated on contact with Bob's head, the effect of being bashed with it night after night soon took its toll. After 21 performances, Bob's doctor diagnosed concussion and ordered him to stop. Bob said, 'I just don't know how John Wayne does it.'

* * *

Glaswegian actor Jimmy Twaddale got commendably tied up in his part when he had to wear a straitjacket in the aptly named play A *Sense Of Freedom*. Jimmy was portraying ex-prisoner Jimmy Boyle at the Odyssey Theatre Company in North London, and wanted to do Boyle proud. So, as the part required being trussed up for a while, Twaddale stayed behind after rehearsals one night to practise wriggling free from his canvas confines. All the other actors had left except Scott Forrest who strapped Jimmy into the jacket, which encased him from head to foot, and then popped downstairs for a pint in the pub. Back upstairs, Jimmy had little luck in getting out of the straitjacket, and waited patiently for Scott to return. Unfortunately, Scott, having finished his drink, had forgotten all about Jimmy and had set off home to bed. Finally, when Jimmy realised what had happened, he started to shout for help. He shouted for the whole of Saturday night and all through Sunday, but to no avail. On Monday morning the producer Liam Dale arrived to find Jimmy still rolling about on the floor. That evening Jimmy gave a performance which he said was 'full of real feeling'.

* * *

The woman in the rear stalls was engrossed in *Illuminations*, a play about the Labour party at the Lyric, Hammersmith, when she suffered a heart attack. The call went up for a doctor in the house, and a man climbed over several seats to get to her. Had the woman been well enough to notice, she would probably have appreciated the somewhat surreal coincidence – it was none other than David Owen! He stayed with her until an ambulance arrived.

*   *   *

Japanese tycoon Zenya Hamada was once described as the oriental answer to Shakespeare. Hamada, 66, made his name and money from a chain of golf clubs in his native country, then turned his hand to writing plays. He took one of his *oeuvre*, *The Atom Bomb*, to the Edinburgh Festival, where he then sacked his entire cast of seven on the basis that they were too good! He claimed that there was a real danger of the audience applauding. One of the seven to be shown the door was actor David McKail, who has appeared in *Lovejoy*. Out, but not down, he commented, 'Mr Hamada was totally inscrutable. We thought maybe we were misunderstanding him. He has a problem articulating English.' The second cast was hastily recruited from a Glasgow agency. Mr Hamada explained briefly, 'Last actors ignored director so I fired them. New actors great. This will be number one show in Festival.' To make sure of this, Hamada gave away all the tickets. Yet even this gesture was not always enough to ensure an audience in his native Japan, where Hamada has been known to be the sole audience member in his Tokyo theatre. Still, Hamada remains optimistic about his future: 'I'm like Van Gogh. He didn't sell a painting until he was dead. I, too, will be famous only after my death.'

* * *

Richard Burton, when making the film *The Assassination of Trotsky* with Alain Delon, had to warn the Frenchman about his over-enthusiastic use of the ice-axe. 'Careful,' Burton said. 'There may be plenty of French actors around, but kill me and you've killed a sixth of the world's Welsh actors.'

* * *

The 1981 book *Great Operatic Disasters* recounts the sad fate suffered by a soprano who made the crucial error of getting on the stage hands' nerves. The opera was *Tosca*, playing to a packed audience in New York, and the boys had fallen out in a big way with the prima donna-ish diva. At the end of the performance, when Tosca flings herself from the castle battlements, this singer found that instead of landing on the usual mattress, she fell on to a trampoline . . . Audience members recall her bouncing back into view a dozen times or more before the curtain finally fell.

* * *

Ingrid Bergman said the greatest piece of acting advice she ever received came from Alfred Hitchcock. In the middle of a heated debate over a scene that she complained she couldn't do naturally, Hitchcock yelled in exasperation, 'All right, if you can't do it naturally, fake it!'

* * *

Shaw Taylor, the presenter of *Police Five* remembers one Leicester theatrical landlady especially well. Every morning as she was dishing up breakfast, she seemed to know exactly who had been seeing whom during the night and would comment, 'Well, you two seemed to have a good time last night.' Shaw worked out that she had wired the lights in her house like a burglar alarm system so she could detect lights going on and off, and keep electronic tabs on her lodgers.

*   *   *

Politics provokes performers into some of the greatest outbreaks of luvviness. One well-known actress sought a quiet spot to read her copy of the *Guardian* during a break in filming. A colleague, seeing her look highly emotional, asked her what was wrong. 'It's so terrible,' she gulped, tears rolling from her large eyes. 'There are three million unemployed people in Britain.' Another time, Sammy Davis Jnr. surprised the world of showbiz when he claimed to be too distressed by Senator Robert Kennedy's death to continue with his show at the London Palladium. Oddly enough, Davis had managed to continue on the night that his own mother had died.

*   *   *

Glenda Jackson was accused of having only been successful in gaining her Hampstead seat because of her fame as an actress. In her own defence, Glenda dismissed such a notion. She suggested gamely that she had lost an equal number of votes from people who did not like her acting.

*   *   *

During the making of a Roman epic, Victor Mature slipped out to a Los Angeles bar for a quick drink with some fellow actors, striding into the bar in full Roman armour. The barman stood staring at them, speechless. 'What's the matter?' complained Mature. 'Don't you serve members of the armed forces?'

*　　*　　*

Director Billy Wilder had some problems with Marilyn Monroe in *Some Like It Hot*; basically, she was incapable of learning her lines. In one scene, she was required to enter a room and take a slug of whisky from a bottle in a drawer, then speak a line of dialogue. By take number 53, Wilder was reduced to placing a piece of paper with the line written on it in every drawer in the cabinet. Assured of success, Marilyn was confident at last ... she went straight to the wrong piece of furniture.

*　　*　　*

Glenda Jackson was fractionally less self-deprecating when someone asked her a question about directors. Snorting in disgust, she said, 'I have worked with so few directors worthy of that name that I don't have sufficient experience to help with the inquiry.' Pausing for a moment, she then added, 'and I have worked with a great many who have no right to the name "director".' She was, of course, not referring to director Sir Peter Hall, who once remarked that he'd had to teach actors for six weeks before rehearsals started, adding, 'That's not uncommon.' Neither could she conceivably have had in mind Jonathan Miller, who once said that certain opera stars were dim-witted celebrities who stuck with a certain version of a performance simply because they had done it time and time again. He added bluntly, 'They are famous for their singing and they're buggered if they're going to do any smart-arsed idea that you have got as a director. If you have what Coral Browne (the actress) once described as "two hundredweight of condemned veal" you don't direct it. You simply transport it.'

* * *

P. G. O'Rourke once said there were three types of actresses: the silly, the very silly, and Shirley MacLaine.

* * *

One of the jokes circulating round the backstages of theatres of the West End summed up the nature of actors everywhere. Stage hands were to be found giggling over the following: How many actors does it take to change a light bulb? Answer: Twenty – one to put it in and the other 19 to stand round and say, 'That could have been me.'

* * *

Maggie Smith, playing Desdemona to Laurence Olivier's Othello, got her own back for his constant references to her pronunciation. On stage the duo achieved dramatic brilliance, but backstage the relationship was slightly strained. Maggie, taking note of his suggestions about her vowel sounds, swore to get even. The opportunity arose when, as was customary, Olivier was sitting in his dressing-room pre-performance, practising his own vowels. Alerted by the low mooing sounds coming from his dressing-room, Maggie flung open the door and announced with perfect intonation, 'How now, brown cow.' But she got more that she bargained for – Olivier was sitting there completely starkers!

* * *

When Tatum O'Neal was 14 and making *International Velvet*, a school inspector visiting the set noted that her maths was very poor. He asked whether that bothered her. 'Oh, no,' Tatum replied, 'I have an accountant.'

*　　*　　*

In a variation on bishop/actress jokes, leading ladies were called in to help vicars add a bit of drama to their sermons. At Salisbury Theological College, trainee vicars were given lessons on breathing and pronunciation in an attempt to lure more people away from the Sunday papers and into church. Actress Sonia Clissold, who played the part of Ros Plimmer in the TV series *Casualty*, was roped in to teach the ordinands. She revealed such hot tips as, 'Your breath is going to spread like a melting Mars Bar on a radiator. If you have had eight pints of beer you will not have the space for breath. You cannot breathe correctly and preach well on a full stomach.' She also advised preachers to have a good yawn before embarking on sermons, as it would relax their vocal chords. Accoustics were dealt with too. Sonia suggested that saying 'Jesus Christ' should not sound like 'Jeser Chrise'. She added, 'You need to cut the S off smartly and make a good crisp T.'

*　　*　　*

The beautiful Italian actress Gina Lollobrigida

had an interesting time working with Sean Connery in *Woman of Straw*. Planning to give his leading lady a small stage 'tap', Connery, obviously not aware of his own strength, gave her the sort of left hook Frank Bruno would not have been ashamed of. Gina's mouth was cut and her face swelled up, and filming had to be postponed until she had recovered. Connery, who has expressed his belief in giving women the odd whack, admitted that this particular slap had turned into more of a 'fair belt'. A bruised Gina added, 'We had done the scene 10 times without accident. One cannot control these things – and usually they don't hurt. But this time the slap was a few inches out – and I really felt it.'

*　　*　　*

Wolf Mankowitz decided not to take the negative reviews of his musical *Belle* lying down. After one especially vicious write-up by a critic, he retaliated by sending a little something to the reviewer's Fleet Street office … he had four showgirls deliver a coffin.

*　　*　　*

Peter Sellers, while making *The Mask Behind the Mask*, had so many roles, he showed signs of forgetting who he really was. Approached by a studio hand who asked, 'Are you Peter Sellers?' he replied absent-mindedly, 'Not today.'

* * *

During the making of *Lawrence of Arabia*, Peter O'Toole discovered that camels were definitely not darlings to work with. Injuries he sustained during filming in the Jordanian desert included several concussions, a dislocated spine, a sprained neck, a cracked ankle bone and torn ligaments. Perhaps the most painful mishap was the loss of use of several fingers due to a camel bite. O'Toole later admitted that although he had clocked up 1,000 hours on the backs of various camels, he hated the creatures. He said, 'I couldn't stand the sight nor the smell of them. They skinned the hide off me. They spat at me, bit me and paralysed my fingers. But I decided, if I'm going to play Lawrence I've got to ride like him.' During filming, water supplies had to be brought in by lorry, which made the cost of a bath around £100 a time! O'Toole also had to learn how to deal with the sandstorm scenes. Some had to be repeated as often as 25 times, before he could act without blinking against the onslaught of sand and sun. 'I hate weather of all kinds, and positively loathe any kind of sport that involves me. I felt anything but a hero,' said heroic O'Toole.

*   *   *

Jose Ferrer had to play the part of the crippled French painter Toulouse-Lautrec in the Moulin Rouge. For the sake of verisimilitude, Ferrer shuffled round for hours on his knees. He practised on the Parisian pavements by strapping his shoes to his knees and sliding along, but admitted that it hurt tremendously. 'The pain became killing after 20 minutes. And when I stood up it got worse.'

Sir Alec Guinness blamed his baldness on a close shave he had for a part as a Chinese coolie in a play. Having removed all his hair, it never grew back properly. Bette Davis plucked her eyebrows out to get into her screen role of Queen Elizabeth I. Lon Chaney took the compulsion to get it right one stage further: so anxious was he to be convincing as Quasimodo in the original 1923 silent version of *The Hunchback of Notre Dame* that he insisted on wearing a straitjacket. He decided that even this didn't give him enough physical grotesqueness, so he pulled his own shoulder out of joint. It left him with a permanent injury.

*   *   *

Boris Karloff, better known as Frankenstein's monster, used to have to spend eight hours being made up for his part in the 1931 horror film. The total weight of that make-up was 50 pounds. The following year, in his role in *The Mummy*, he had to have cotton threads stuck on to his face which were then treated with two dozen types of paint and clay. To finish the mummy fixation effect, 200 yards of bandages were wrapped around his body. Karloff joked, 'My greatest ordeal was getting it off without ripping half my face away.' But these make-up ordeals were nothing compared to the time he grew a beard and then had the rest of his face covered in fish scales . . .

* * *

Axl Rose, lead singer of the group Guns N' Roses, will reputedly not play in any town that starts with the letter M; he believes the letter to be cursed.

* * *

Mr T, who played in *The A-Team* and *Rocky* III, is another performer who believes in getting exactly what he wants. To get into the right artistic frame of mind to play in the 1980s adventure series T *and* T, Mr T issued a list of non-refusable requests. First he asked for a mobile home with hot and cold running water, a fan and humidifier, blankets, towels and 100 per cent cotton sheets. The fridge had to be stocked with fried chicken, beef and turkey, chicken soup, egg and tuna fish salads, bran muffins, cashew nuts and fruit juice. Next, all his flights had to be booked on United or American Airlines. Mr T had to have his clothes dry-cleaned or washed every 24 hours, and a wardrobe assistant to arrange his clothes in the trailer before he got there to dress himself. Also enshrined in the contract was a clause relating to his preference for not being close to tactile people. It said: 'Mr T doesn't want to be touched a lot and he doesn't want anybody doing anything to his hair.' The only exception to this rule came in the form of the weekly massages which Mr T ordered. Oh, and the driver of the white limo that drove him to and from the set every day was – rather generously – allowed to say good morning, but then could only speak when spoken to. Finally, there was the matter of the £175 daily allowance which Mr T asked for and received!

*   *   *

Mr T's contract riders were positively modest in comparison to Frank Sinatra's. Sinatra encapsulated this special interpretation of *My Way* in a 23-page list of requirements for his dressing-room. These included a selection of spirits – Jack Daniels, Chivas Regal, Absolut vodka, Beefeater gin, Courvoisier Cognac, bottles of red and white wine and an ice-bucket. When he got peckish, the singer liked to be able to choose from twelve tubes of cherry-flavoured Life-Saver sweets, three cans of chicken and rice soup (plus a primus stove to heat it up on) two egg salad sandwiches, a bag of chocolate rolls and a full cheeseboard. Sundries had not been forgotten either: a carton of untipped Camel cigarettes were stipulated, together with six boxes of Kleenex, linen napkins, throat lozenges, cotton wool, aftershave, news-papers, books, shampoo and soap. Oh – and toothpicks.

*　　*　　*

Before appearing at London's Victoria Palace Theatre in *The Little Foxes* in 1982, Elizabeth Taylor insisted on having her dressing-room completely redecorated. It wasn't just that she wanted the walls changed to match her violet eyes – she also wanted a huge fish-tank complete with violet tropical fish, violet carpet and a fresh supply of violets delivered daily to her door.

*　　*　　*

Bonnie Langford followed suit by having her dressing-room decked out in baby-doll pink whilst appearing in *Me and My Girl* at the Adelphi Theatre, London in 1987. Bonnie then added the finishing touches – frilly pink curtains and a little pink wastepaper bin. Country and Western singer Hank Wangford had simpler taste. He just demanded that a cactus was placed in his dressing-room before he went on stage. Rolling Stone Bill Wyman had it written into his contract that whenever he appeared, not only must there be a ping-pong table on hand, but a crew member good enough to take him on at the game. Eartha Kitt went one further by asking, not for one but two chorus boys to be at her disposal. Eartha needed squash partners and because she is so fit, she likes to take on two people at once! Alan Alda, star of MASH, likes to eat fresh pasta when on set . . . so much so that he takes his own pasta-making machine wherever he goes. Dillie Keane, star of many West End musicals, once had it written into her contract that she had to have two items delivered to her dressing-room every night: the first was a bottle of Australian Chardonnay, the second, a packet of sequins.

*   *   *

During one rehearsal, Toscanini flew into a rage

with a violinist and ordered him from the stage. As the player reached the exit he yelled across the hall, 'Nuts to you!'. The conductor looked up and snarled, 'It's too late to apologise.'

* * *

Lauren Bacall was touring Australia in *Sweet Bird of Youth* during the 1980's. Discovering that she had left an important parcel behind in Melbourne, she sent a crew member back from Sydney to pick it up. When the precious cargo was hand-delivered to her it turned out to be a jar of black olives which she had brought over from the States.

* * *

In one production of Timberlake Wertenbaker's *Our Country's Good*, such was the shortage of men to play the parts of officers, that all the available women had to fill these military roles. Producer Max Stafford-Clark said, 'We had a prize each evening for the most butch man on stage – and it wasn't always necessarily won by a woman.'

* * *

Snow White and the Seven Dwarfs presents an annual

financial headache for hard-up theatre companies. If only the story had starred a slightly less lavish number of the vertically challenged! Not only are miniature actors few and far between, but they also come at the full-sized price – and often more. You have to have every sympathy with dwarf actors, since there aren't too many suitable shows for them (in fact that's the only one that springs to mind) but it is not hard either to see the theatre management's predicament. The solution is often to try to economise. Thus every Christmas you will find a Dopey and a Grumpy running on stage, and then the lights dimming before the (non-existent) rest of the gang can be seen. Or Sneezy and Happy will run amok amongst the other actors, praying that the audience, confused by the commotion, will think there are more of them. Actor Mr George Claydon, just 50 inches tall, put the case forward for the dramatic realism that only the correct number of dwarfs can provide. He said, 'You cannot beat the appearance of real dwarfs marching along behind Snow White with that "Hi-ho, hi-ho, it's off to work we go" routine. How on earth can you have a production which comes down to Snow White and the Three Dwarfs?' he demanded. The then editor of *The Stage* magazine, Peter Hepple, could only think of one instance where the number of dwarfs had been reduced. Apparently, one financially bereft touring production of the play had only two dwarfs … who would come on stage each night, calling behind them, 'Come on lads.'

* * *

Diners at a Torquay restaurant were treated to an impromptu performance when a waitress was asked to audition for a lead role in a bedroom farce while dishing up the food. Sue Boyd, 36, was asked to try for the part of a leggy blonde German seductress by a dining director. The amused audience applauded Sue's rendition of the part and she got the job.

* * *

The rarefied atmosphere of Glyndebourne was shattered when two opera singers fell out and started a punch-up. Opera singer David Ellis lunged at tenor Kurt Streit for what he thought was over-indulging in a stage kiss with his girl-friend, soprano Amanda Roocroft.

* * *

Actor Nicol Williamson fell out with his American co-star in one production of Hamlet. The two could not be reconciled when their backstage discussion about different methods of acting turned into an on-stage battle. Williamson smacked his co-star with the flat of his sword mid-performance, yelled, 'Put some life into it,' and then watched as the co-star left the stage and refused to return. The play became a cult success, known unofficially as I *Hate Hamlet*, and went on to play to packed houses.

* * *

In 1894 thespian rivalry between another Brit/Yank duo ended in actual bloodshed, when Edwin Foreet and William Charles Macready came to loggerheads on stage. Their supporters battled it out leaving, according to one unlikely contemporary account, a death toll of 34 with a further 100 injured!

* * *

Abraham Lincoln, looking forward to a quiet evening at the theatre, was confronted by the mad actor John Wilkes Booth who wanted to settle the score for his side's defeat in the civil war. He leaped on stage and shot Lincoln dead, screaming, 'Death to all tyrants.' As he did so he fell and broke his leg.

* * *

To avoid moving from boarding house to boarding house whilst performing on tour, comedian Eric Morecambe invested in a caravan for his wife Joan and their daughter Gail. Joan remembers that one day she was cooking a casserole on a Calor gas stove when she noticed that the flame had gone out. Without thinking she struck a match and there was an almighty explosion. Gail's highchair was lifted 2 feet off the ground and Joan's hair caught fire. Eric arrived home just in time to see his wife beating out the flames. Approaching her he said, 'Who are you?'

*   *   *

In 1735, tempestuous actor Charles Macklin hit fellow thespian Thomas Hallam with a cane after an argument about a wig. The cane hit Hallam in the eye and he died a day later.

*   *   *

Actor Alan Devlin was a bit shaky on the first verse of 'I Am A Ruler of the Queen's Navy', his opening song in HMS *Pinafore* at Dublin's Gaiety Theatre. He stumbled through the second verse and then announced to the audience, 'Oh bugger this, I'm off home.' He then stalked off stage past the audience and out of the door. Within minutes of this unscripted departure, Devlin's understudy was carrying on where he left off, minus the expletives. A theatre spokesman added later, 'You could say Devlin's balance wasn't the best and he was taken ill.' None too surprisingly, it was also announced that Devlin, an ex-member of the Royal Shakespeare Company, would not be continuing with the show. Later at home, Devlin admitted that he was thinking of giving up the boards for good. He added, 'I don't think acting suits me.'

* * *

The theatre critic of the *Financial Times* caused a rumpus when he complained that an actress playing a Greek goddess hadn't shaved her armpits. Michael Coveney, who had seen the RSC's production of *Pericles* at the Swan Theatre, in which unshaven actress Sally Edwards had performed, wrote: 'I know it's none of my business really, but I do think the goddess Diana would have shaved her armpits before entering her temple at Ephesus.' Coveney later admitted that he had understood that the 'remark didn't go down too well at the RSC'. Whilst the actress concerned didn't comment herself, her colleague Imelda Staunton fumed, 'It's none of Coveney's business. It's so personal.' Actress Susan

Hampshire, commenting on the issue, said thoughtfully, 'Perhaps the thinking actress doesn't shave her armpits any more, although it's a very personal choice for the individual concerned. I've known a Shakespearean leading lady who went on with hairy legs as well as hairy armpits.' Coveney meanwhile stormed on. 'It seems to be a tribal rite of these feminists not to shave their armpits.' A classics lecturer at Cambridge University, the not inaptly named Dr Mary Beard, supported the critic's opinion. Dr Beard added, 'One of the first principles of Greek culture is that men are hairy and women are soft and smooth: classical goddesses are not troubled with hairy armpits.' Then, attempting to give a contemporary parallel, she added, 'It's like the Queen not needing to pee.'

*　　*　　*

In 1973, a performance of *The Dirtiest Show in Town* at the Duchess Theatre, London had to be stopped for a quarter of an hour, whilst 9 police officers escorted almost the entire first two rows of the audience outside. The 27 men had apparently got the subtle message conveyed by the show's title, but had taken it a tad too seriously. They refused a request for them to leave the theatre after their comments and raucous jokes had upset the sensitivities of the cast. The worst thing for the actors was that the rest of the audience gave every indication of finding the men's interjections funnier than the show!

* * *

Rachael Kempson, wife of Sir Michael Redgrave and mother of Vanessa, Lynn and Corin, once leapt off the stage and laid into two young men in the audience at a production of A *Sense Of Detachment*. Other members of the cast shouted at Miss Kempson, then 62, to stop beating up the men, but one actress, Denise Coffey, whose tender love scene had just been ruined by the duo's comments, egged her on with the rallying cry of, 'Go on Rachael!' Later, Kempson announced to her fellow actors, 'I was very annoyed for all of you. I did it on our behalf.' She explained, 'I saw red. I am not a bad-tempered person, though I do get nervous. But we were all pretty tired by this time and I jumped off the stage and hit both of them. Of course one should not do this sort of thing, but once in a blue moon you do.' Describing the irritants, the assailant said, 'They were just a couple of show-offs, very well-dressed and in the most expensive seats. I think the cast cried out for me to stop because they were afraid that the men would hit back.' The two young men should not have been astonished by the star's sudden offensive – as it happens, the play involves two actors who sit in the audience and make remarks on the entertainment.

*   *   *

A charity concert almost ended in a full-scale brawl when an on-stage comedian and a member of the audience came to blows. The unseemly business was at the London Roundhouse in 1972, at a concert named 'The Greasy Truckers Grand Opening Party' which was aiming to raise money for a community centre. The problem started when an American comedian called Uncle Dirty was riled by a heckler in the front row. The youth then jumped on the stage and went for Uncle Dirty, who was the last person to approach in this way, since he had just come out of the US Army. Uncle Dirty knocked the heckler to the floor before he could throw the first punch. Then, as friends of the now unconscious complainant tried to get him off-stage, other members of the audience fought to hold them back. It resulted in 8 of the audience being treated for cuts and bruises in the theatre's first-aid room. Uncle Dirty's manager commented, 'All hell broke loose ... I've never seen anything like it in a British theatre.' Which only makes one wonder whether it was a common occurrence at Uncle Dirty's performances else-where ...

* * *

Never was the old saying about not acting with animals or children more apt than at a Bournemouth production of *Carmen*, where a dog somehow found its way on to the stage during the smugglers' scene. It stayed there placidly enough, disregarded by the cast, until it spotted the conductor's baton. Impatient with waiting for the conductor to throw it for him, the dog started barking very loudly. Only when his barks drowned out everything else did the stage manager order the curtain to be dropped. Another unexpected extra, this time in a production of *The Bed-Sitting Room* starring Spike Milligan at the Saville Theatre, was dealt with in a very different way. Halfway through the play, a poet identifying himself as Mike Granger jumped out of the audience and on to the stage. Shouting to Spike, 'Here I am!' he climbed into the prop bed and stayed there for the duration of the performance.

* * *

Perhaps it was and perhaps it wasn't a bad idea to use a live donkey for an operatic production in that seismologically challenged city, San Francisco. As the soprano was making her entrance in a cart pulled by the poor beast, a minor earth tremor sent him into spasm. With all regard for the diva forgotten, the donkey shot off across the stage, causing the singer to be turfed out on to the boards and most of the scenery to collapse. A less sensitive donkey had to be found for the following performance.

* * *

The dignity of a 1962 performance of *Hamlet* was saved by the cool behaviour of a girl sitting in the front stalls. During the duel between Hamlet and Laertes, Hamlet was a little over-zealous in disarming his opponent and ended up flicking his rapier right into the lap of the young theatre-goer. Without batting an eyelid, the girl stood up and with a gracious gesture returned the rapier to Hamlet. The fight continued, and when the cast took their curtain calls, Hamlet blew the young lady a kiss.

* * *

Eugen Carle was taking part in a comedy alongside his friend Emil Hermann at a theatre in the Black Forest, Germany. The final scene of the play was a duel scene in which Emil shoots Eugen. The scene over, the audience was in raptures and the curtain went down, while the cast waited for Eugen to get up off the floor. Then someone noticed the pool of blood under his body. When Emil realised what he had done he fled, to be found hours later, sobbing in a barn. It transpired that Eugen had himself loaded the gun and, in his nervousness, had mistaken live bullets for blanks. Luckily for Emil, there were scores of witnesses.

*　　*　　*

In 1960 Jane Fonda made her debut in the film *The Tall Story*, as a giggling teenager with a crush on a baseball player. The critics responded by prophesying that she was unlikely to follow in her father's footsteps. Jane herself was far more philosophical about the role. She said later, 'The movie was so bad, there was nowhere for me to go after that but up!'

*　　*　　*

Oscar-winning heart-throb Kevin Costner had a chequered career before films like *Dances With Wolves* made him a box-office smash. In fact, Costner refuses to talk about the teenage sex film in which he first starred. The film itself was a flop, but even so, rare copies of it still change hands for large sums in the States. Costner's next attempt to win favour with Hollywood was *The Big Chill*. Whilst the film itself fared much better at the box-office, Costner's role as a dead body was consigned to the cutting-room floor.

* * *

Anjelica Huston refused to work for 16 years after critics rated her debut performance in *Walk With Love* 'supremely inept'. Meanwhile it was only a bet which led Mr Crocodile Dundee himself, Paul Hogan, to become a star. Hogan entered TV talent show *New Faces* as a dare with his tap-dancing/knife-throwing routine. Oddly enough, he only came second, but shortly afterwards his career took off.

* * *

Rather than facing endless rounds of sandwiches, members of The Shanghai Kunju Theatre Company ordered a consignment of 4,000 Pot Noodles to accompany them on their three-month tour round Britain. It seems they hadn't heard that Chinese restaurants are becoming quite common in Britain.

* * *

Punk actress Barbara Adside, who has appeared in episodes of TV serial *Cagney and Lacey*, revealed that she was born with no legs as a result of spina bifida. 'I'm more versatile than a regular actress,' she bravely explained when the story came out. Because of my three sets of artificial legs my height varies from 5 foot 3 inches to 5 foot 5 inches to 5 foot 7 inches. That means I can act opposite either a short or a tall leading man.'

* * *

A double-glazing firm started advertising for out of work actors to sell their product, on the grounds that a theatrical training came in handy when persuading people to buy windows. The firm, Everest, put their ads in the acting magazine *The Stage*, offering those 'resting' the opportunity to earn up to £800 a week. The actors' union Equity, with 80 per cent of its members out of work, backed the idea.

* * *

Screen goddess Joan Crawford made a porn movie in 1924, called *The Casting Couch*, in which she performed explicit sex acts with a film producer. When Crawford finally found stardom she spent thousands trying to buy up all the existing copies.

* * *

American author Arthur Meyer wrote a book called *The Ghosts Of the Rich And Famous*, which claimed amongst other things that the spirit of Judy Garland was trapped in a New York lightbulb. Meyer went on to assert that Clark Gable and his actress lover Carole Lombard were still going strong despite the extreme downer of being dead; Errol Flynn, deceased for some 30 years, was still frequenting his old Hollywood haunts; the spirit of John Lennon was still working for peace, and Marilyn Monroe had sent messages saying that her death was an accident and not suicide.

* * *

Veteran director Alfred Hitchcock asserted that the love action amongst the luvvies doesn't always stop when the director shouts 'Cut'. Hitchcock, then 71, added: 'Most actors and actresses have love affairs with their co-stars. It's human nature.' He continued, 'When you've got a love scene going at four in the afternoon, it finishes in the dressing-room after six. They can't help it. Sometimes it's a temporary affair, lasting just an hour, with them hating each other afterwards. They may go from picture to picture doing that. Sometimes it becomes permanent.' This constant changing of partners was the reason for the high divorce rate in Hollywood, said the legendary man. He elucidated, 'They believe in the love scenes they're playing. I remember one kissing scene. It was so real we could hardly get them apart! Two other stars were total strangers before they met for a love scene. Now they have a baby and haven't got married.' Despite his forthright views, Hitchcock maintained that what the stars did was none of his business: 'I'm an onlooker. It's the business of the priest and the censor, not me.'

*　　*　　*

Kevin Costner had the pleasure of making out in the back of a taxi with beautiful actress Sean Young in the film *No Way Out*. Kevin admitted, 'Look, we're all red-blooded dudes. And if someone strips off, there comes a point where you have to look.' Sean, on the other hand, was busy asking how many members of the crew had had similar escapades in the rear seats of a taxi. She said, 'Just about everyone had except me.'

*　　*　　*

Jerry Zucker, director of the blockbusting film

Ghost, starring Demi Moore and Patrick Swayze, had his own opinion of why the famous love scene around the potter's wheel proved to be so effective. Ignoring the blatant sex-appeal of the two stars, Zucker confided, 'It proved to be such a hot, sexy scene, there was no need to use the other love scene we had originally shot. Clay is just so sexy.'

* * *

Video producer Robin Ware of Newport in Shropshire came up with a novel idea for screen-struck women. For a mere £300, he offered them the chance to be the heroines in their own film, which would be shot by a professional crew. Customers provided their own storyline and actors – and naturally took the leading role themselves. The idea was designed for women who wanted to re-enact their favourite scenes from romantic novels. Robin commented, 'There'll be nothing saucy. It'll be in the best possible taste.'

* * *

Mel Gibson described the scene in which he shared a steam bath with Michelle Pfeiffer in *Tequila Sunrise* as 'really a hot hot-tub scene'. Mel also admitted that he and co-star Kurt Russell had decided that Pfeiffer was too thin for the sex scene and had forced her to eat chocolates on the grounds that she needed 'an extra five pounds'.

*　　*　　*

Raquel Welch started off her career as a secretary to a San Diego bishop when she was just 19. There she was spotted by a sculptor whose forte was religious statues. Convinced that Ms Welch bore a resemblance to the Virgin Mary (she fell for that old line), he persuaded her to pose for him. Shortly afterwards the statue appeared, peering down from a building in the centre of the city.

*　　*　　*

Before Clint Eastwood transformed himself into Dirty Harry, he had a mélange of menial jobs. After leaving school, Clint worked as a lumberjack and fought forest fires. Then he landed a job at a furnace company in Texas, of which he said, 'The heat got so intense you felt as though your skin would peel right off your body.' Trying to cool off after that experience, Clint became a Texan lifeguard who also gave swimming lessons. Other stars had even more inauspicious starts to their careers: Tina Turner was a cotton picker and a practical nurse assistant; Rod Stewart had a spell of gravedigging at London's Highgate Cemetary; Tracey Ullman sang backing vocals for Bonnie Langford; Terry Wogan was a cashier for the Royal Bank Of Ireland in Dublin: Griff Rhys Jones was a minder for the Sheikh of Qatar; Julie Walters trained as a nurse; Goldie Hawn was a go-go dancer; Kenneth Branagh was a children's book reviewer on the Reading *Evening Post*; Nigel Havers was a cellarman in a wine shop and then a researcher on the *Jimmy Young Show*; Jonathan Ross was the child who advertised Kellogg's Rice Krispies on TV.

* * *

A group of travelling actors once took their production of *Hamlet* to a quiet country village. Emotions were running high amongst the troupe because their wages had not been paid for some time. The performance however was going swingingly until Hamlet had to pose the question about his father's ghost. 'Perchance,' said Hamlet dramatically, 'Twill walk again.' His query was answered by a loud voice of dissatisfaction from off-stage: 'Nay, 'twill walk no more until its salary is paid.'

* * *

The British playwright Christopher Hampton once likened asking an actor what he thinks about critics to 'asking a lamppost how it feels about dogs'.

*   *   *

Talking of critics, a reviewer once gave his opinion on a performance of Uncle Tom's Cabin which had been flamboyantly staged using no less than 50 actors and 10 real bloodhounds. The critic wrote: 'The dogs gave an excellent performance, but received little support from the rest of the company.' Another reviewer let his feelings be known about a new play called Wham!. The review which appeared the following day read simply: 'Ouch!'

*   *   *

It is not known whether this is an apocryphal story, a true tale or a theatrical joke: A couple of comedians who were down on their luck were trying to make their way to Ireland. At Holyhead they persuaded a skipper to let them board his cargo boat. When the boat arrived in Dublin the skipper was asked by customs officers what he had on board. 'A load of guano and a couple of actors,' the skipper replied. Turning to his friend, one of the actors complained, 'Aren't we ever going to top the bill?'

3
The Roar of the Greasepaint . . . Amateur Night

The first performance by some Sheffield morris dancers in Equador, South America was almost scuppered by the fickle finger of fashion. The dancers were faced with the awesome task of finding 40 pairs of buttoned braces in a hurry just before they set off in August 1993 for a three-week international folk-dancing festival in Quito. On a routine visit to a Sheffield department store to pick up the dark blue braces – the elastic in their old ones was sagging – troupe spokesman Peter Smith, a 46-year-old college lecturer, met with the shock response: 'We don't stock them any more. They've gone out of fashion.' Mr Smith appealed to the *Yorkshire Evening Post* for help. 'We are the first British morris side to visit the country,' he explained, 'and we want to look our best. What makes it awkward is that we don't want the modern clip-ons.'

*   *   *

A young boy in a school nativity play, miffed that he had been superseded for the part of Joseph, had to content himself with the role of Innkeeper. Answering the knock on the door, he opened it and surveyed the couple hovering expectantly on the doorstep. After a moment or two and in a voice which carried right to the back row, he announced politely, 'Mary, you can come in. Joseph, you can buzz off.'

*   *   *

The chorus set the scene for the entrance of the King. 'It's the Prince, His Highness,' they trilled. Right on cue came His Royalness, in an outfit fit for a king. Unfortunately, as he walked on stage the right Royal wig caught on a nail protruding from the scenery and swung there in a most un-regal manner. His Highness had no choice but to continue, with the spotlight glaring off his bald head.

*   *   *

At the youth club panto in Chesham, Buckinghamshire, the Queen of Hearts popped a tray of delicious looking tarts into an oven that promptly exploded. There was a deafening bang and the Queen was catapulted to the other side of the stage where she landed among some props.

*　*　*

The reputedly jinxed play *The Ghost Train*, written by ex-*Dad's Army* star Arnold Ridley, created mayhem at a village production in Holybourne, Hampshire. Whilst the spooky play was running, the leading lady Vivien Riley dislocated a knee, two other actors sprained their ankles, another actor caught glandular fever and the director was bruised after a fall. One actress caught flu, another actor's car was broken into, and on stage, crockery fell off the kitchen shelf. Added to this, a ghostly figure was seen loitering in the wings. The show's producer vowed, 'We'll never do it again.'

*　*　*

An amateur production in Derbyshire provided most of its drama before the curtain was even raised. The problem came in the form of a local PE teacher, cast as a female wrestler. Miss Carolyn Garrod, 30, who described herself as 'a big softie', started by injuring the producer in rehearsals with a drop kick. Next to go was a designer, whom Miss Garrod left with a cracked collar-bone. Sarah Buck, a 17-year-old member of the cast, counted herself lucky for walking away with only a broken collar-bone after another of Miss Garrod's manoeuvres, known as the 'Irish whip'. Fellow actor Paul Jackson was spared with only broken toes. The leading man injured his knee as another move went amiss, and even the stage referee, acted by Jake Bannister, collapsed after being held in a rather effective little head lock. Despite this splendid injury list, Miss Garrod rejected the local suggestions that she should quit teaching for a career in wrestling.

* * *

In one production of *Samson and Delilah*, Samson took his role just that bit too seriously. He leaned so heavily against a temple pillar that it gave way, came tumbling down and struck him a glancing blow. This Samson ended up in hospital with concussion. On the other hand, actors can also suffer when scenery refuses to budge. One amateur, whose only line was 'Mercy, mercy the house is collapsing' found himself repeating the line *ad nauseum* as stage hands struggled behind the set, trying to get the ceiling to collapse.

* * *

During an amateur production of an opera the conductor gave one singer his cue by pointing at him. The singer, overcome by first-night nerves, jumped, exclaiming, 'Who me?' In another local production an amateur musician gaily played his way through what should have been a dramatic pause in a symphony. Not content with ruining the ambiance, he then shouted to the conductor, 'I say, old man, I'm most frightfully sorry.'

* * *

In an amateur production in Brighton, a couple had just reached the tense moment where they have an emotional debate on whether to elope or not. Before they could reach their decision, however, they were interrupted by an announcement over the public tannoy: 'Will Mrs Jones please come to the manager's office,' a strange voice screeched.

* * *

Jack Fisher put on his wife's clothes to take the lead in a performance of *Hello Dolly* and saved the show. Jack was the producer of Barrow Amateur Operatic Society's big production, so when his wife, the leading lady, collapsed hours before curtain up on the first night, Jack had to step into her shoes. As producer, Jack already knew the songs off by heart and exactly how the part should be interpreted. Luckily, his wife's costume and wigs fitted him perfectly, and he made history as the first man to take the title role, playing the part to acclaim.

* * *

In one production of Iolanthe, a guard had to sing a solo from his sentry box. As he began, he realised that the strap of his busby was slowly riding up his chin. Towards the middle of the song the strap was under his nose and by the end, the poor man was gamely singing away whilst bent double, trying to stop his busby from falling off.

* * *

In Steeple Bumpstead in Essex, Don Thorne got a bit carried away by his star role as Aladdin. Rubbing his lamp with a vengeance, Don conjured up not a gentle genie but a huge flash which left him with a burnt hand. In hospital, Aladdin bumped into Widow Twankey who was there on account of having fallen on stage and dislocated his shoulder. Although the Widow, alias Ian McCrimmons, had sensibly remembered to take off his dress and wig before going to Casualty, he was still in his make-up.

*   *   *

Mary Kitchman of Mulby near York finally hit the big time when she landed a plum role in the village panto. But her first big break turned into just that when a stage trick went horribly wrong. It happened just after the dramatic moment when Mary announces, 'Sailor sail me round'. At this point, two strong members of the cast were to carry out her wishes. But they got overexcited by the bright lights and swung a little too hard. Mary did an involuntary back somersault and ended up meeting the chorus line at short notice. Her injury – a broken collar-bone – meant that Mary had to relinquish her spotlight to her understudy. 'The audience seemed to think it was all part of the show. No one even raised an eyebrow,' she complained later.

*   *   *

One bobby with a penchant for amateur dramatics made his stage debut in a somewhat unconventional manner. It was at a moment of great tension during the Southend Shakespeare Company's performance of *Henry IV, Part One* at the Focus Theatre. Lord Talbot had just cried, 'What stir is this? What tumult in the heavens? Whence cometh this alarum and noise?' when who should step out of the wings but a policeman. Pausing, no doubt for dramatic effect, the constable then delivered his speech with all the emotion he could muster: 'If anybody here has parked on the pavement outside, would they kindly remove their cars. Otherwise I am likely to take action.' Most of the cast stood stunned by this unscripted interruption, while several members of the audience and at least one courtier were seen to make a hurried exit. Later, a spokesman for the Southend police gave a critical review of his colleague's performance by saying, 'Oh dear, how embarrassing. He was probably getting into practice for the Christmas pantomime.'

*　　*　　*

Before he was famous, rock megastar Mark Knopfler of Dire Straits was a trainee reporter on the *Yorkshire Evening Post* in Leeds. One of his earliest assignments was to go to Leeds Railway Station, where the then DJ Jimmy Savile was due to arrive. His instructions were to interview Jimmy. Trying to appear as cool as possible, the scruffy young Knopfler started the interview, 'So, Mr Savile. What brings you to Leeds, then?' Savile looked at the reporter with something between sadness and disdain, and said, 'I live here, ya nit.'

*   *   *

Phil Arthurs had tried his hand at most imper-sonations. Having been the British Elvis Presley and the Singing Rent Collector, Phil's new act was Rocking Gorbachev – a Gorby lookalike who sang rock-and-roll with a Russian accent. Phil even went to the trouble of producing a record called 'Rocking Round The Kremlin' which he hoped would make the Top Ten. When the *Daily Mail* saw photos of Phil in his Gorby get-up, complete with birthmark, they enlisted him to do a nationwide poster campaign. This in turn led Phil to be booked for commercials, trade show openings and the dubious honour of performing on a Spanish TV show, dressed as Gorbachev, imper-sonating Superman singing Elvis Presley songs to a man in drag.

*   *   *

Before the bright lights beckoned Kirstie Alley of

Cheers fame, she worked in a laundry. Kirstie admits that she only applied for the job because she thought it was for the position of receptionist. Therefore, she was rather surprised to find herself toiling in the laundry itself. Alley added, 'It was a bad job. I was there two years and it was always about 130 degrees.'

*　　*　　*

Long before Madonna became a megamusic siren she worked in McDonalds and Burger King for the going rate of $1.50 an hour. Moving onwards and upwards, she then sold ice-cream and had a spell as a coat-check girl. Then she became a painter's model, and also posed for nude photographs. Madonna tried to keep this work in perspective by reminding herself, 'It's for Art . . .'

*　　*　　*

In his early days, Paul McCartney found work with a parcel delivery service called Speedy Prompt Delivery, which required him to sit in the back of a lorry with a pile of parcels. He was laid off after only two weeks and went on to wind electrical coils for the sum of £7 per week.

*　　*　　*

A farmer's daughter gave a rather sharp performance when she landed the role of Margot in an amateur production of *The Desert Song*. In the second act, Jennifer Beak, 22, flung a 3-foot steel sabre down on to the stage. Instead of coming to a halt, the sabre bounced into the air, flew over the footlights and into the orchestra pit. Here it whizzed past the ear of Mr Barry Hartley, the first violinist, and came to rest in his £700 Lucci violin. Barry, describing his ordeal later, said, 'I just saw a flash of steel. As soon as I recovered from the initial shock, the leader handed me a spare violin and everything returned to normal.' Jennifer explained that she had been singing 'What is there to stay my arm from killing the Red Shadow' when the mishap happened, and she had to be given a replacement sword for the next scene. She also added touchingly, 'I'm sorry about the violin.'

*   *   *

Snow White and her seven dwarfs ended up under the stage at a village hall in Devon after their combined weight caused the floor to collapse. It happened when all 28 cast members, including one 18-stone performer, were jumping up and down on the stage in Moretonhampstead. Ron Abraham, who was in charge of the hall, described what happened: 'The back end of the stage dropped about 3 feet, turning it into a kind of ski-slope. Although the cast landed in a great heap, luckily no one was hurt.'

* * *

That fickle prop, the exploding car, lived up to its reputation for making things go with a bang when it backfired violently at a panto in Ashton-under-Lyne, Manchester. The actor at the wheel was hurled out and hit his head on the stage. He ended up in hospital with concussion.

* * *

Amateur actor Mike Raymond was playing the character of Wishy-Washy in a panto in Barnsley when one of the most farcical scenes went badly wrong, and Mike ended up being put through a huge mangle. Despite his experience and the advice of doctors that he should take 3 weeks off to recover, Mike insisted in true showbiz tradition that the show must go on. He was back on stage the following night.

* * *

Theatregoer Jack Hanks got more than a good view when he sat in a front row seat for a production of *Jack and the Beanstalk* performed by the Kilnhurst Amateur Dramatic Society in South Yorkshire. On stage, an actor threw a slice of bread spread thickly with jam at a colleague, who in an ideal world would have prevented it from going any further. The throwee, however, ducked and the bread and jam hit Jack head on. Jack stormed out of the theatre and vowed to send his dry cleaning bill to the producer, Tom Bamford. Mr Bamford was understandably most apologetic. 'We'll certainly pay,' he said.

*　　*　　*

Chris Luby's prowess at impersonating the sounds of the Battle of Britain has taken him far and wide. Chris first discovered his talent for imitating aeroplanes early on in life when, while playing war games with his younger brother, he would become annoyed that his brother's aircraft impersonation was exactly the same as his trains. Many years later, Chris heard a radio documentary about Dunkirk and found he could reproduce a fair likeness of the sound of a German dive-bomber. He went on to extend his repertoire until he could do an entire Second World War bombing raid, starting with a Spitfire taking off over grassy bumps, and continuing with sirens, bombs dropping, incendiaries, night fighters, machine-gun fire and even pilots' radio messages. The whole act lasted for 20 minutes. During the Gulf War, this ultimate amateur act was sent to Saudi Arabia by the Ministry of Defence to entertain the troops. While in Saudi, Chris perfected an impersonation of the Scud missile. He recalls giving a performance at a Royal Air Force Association event. After the show, he was approached in the bar by an old gent who said, 'I say, young man, thought your spitfire was top hole. But by the way, you didn't shut the canopy on take-off.'

4

The Smell of the Crowd . . .
You've Been a Great
Audience

A Broadway audience failed to get into the spirit of a stage version of *The Diary of Anne Frank*. It was almost as if they did not entirely appreciate Pia Zadora's attempt to play the teenage heroine. The audience were already wriggling in their seats when it got to the scene where a group of Gestapo officers enters the Franks' Amsterdam home. As the Nazis sniffed suspiciously around the set, a voice from the rear stalls called out, 'They're in the attic,' and roars of laughter drowned out the play's most dramatic moment.

*   *   *

In 1937, a play at the Lyceum Theatre, London impressed one member of the audience so much that she stood up from her seat in the gallery and gave an impromptu speech of thanks. She explained how much pleasure the play, *Wanted for Murder*, had given her and how, although she had had to travel up from Bournemouth, she would do so again. In response to this eulogy, the principal actor, Mr Terence de Marney turned theatrical tradition on its head by leading the players in a round of applause for the audience.

*   *   *

A grandmother who had been treated to a performance of *The Sound of Music* at Birmingham's Alexandra Theatre was enjoying it so much that she fell asleep in the second half. She woke up in time to see the scene where the former nun Maria marries Captain Von Trapp. However, instead of recognising what was quite clearly a nuptial service, the septegenarian took one look at the host of nuns singing round an altar and thought she had died and gone to heaven. This in itself was quite a shock, but when a stream of Nazi stormtroopers engulfed the stage and started to shout, yell and bark out orders, she reached the worst possible conclusion – in essence, that the bad guys had won the game of life. The grandmother had to be helped out of the theatre by staff to recover. A guilt-ridden Christopher Cazenove, who played the Captain, said afterwards, 'The poor old lady woke up in the middle of a nun's chorus and was convinced that she had gone to meet her maker.'

* * *

Theatregoer Ron Bradbury suffered from a sort of stagefright when he was the sole member of the audience at a production being staged at the Arts Centre in Oldham, Lancashire. It was when Ron surveyed the empty foyer that he realised he was the only one there. If it hadn't been for the usherette who offered to escort him into the auditorium, Ron would have made a dash for it. The curtain rose on 6 actors who were presenting an anthology of Shakespeare, and when it fell again there was silence from the stalls because Ron wasn't certain that the show was over. He admitted, 'It was the most embarrassing moment of my life. In my 45 years of theatregoing I'd never been alone before.' One apparent suggestion as to why the audience was almost non-existent was that John Cleese was appearing in *The Taming of the Shrew* on BBC2.

* * *

Barry Sullivan, an Irish actor famous for his tragic

roles, was once playing Richard the Third. Having uttered the immortal lines, 'A horse! A horse! My kingdom for a horse!' a smart-Aleck from the audience asked whether a jackass wouldn't do just as well. Sullivan, not missing a beat, replied, 'Sure, come around to the stage door at once!'

* * *

Actor Sir Ralph Richardson, taking part in a play's first night, turned to the audience and asked, 'Is there a doctor in the house?' A member of the audience rose at the ready for his moment of medical glory. 'Doctor,' Richardson asked, 'Isn't this play awful?'

* * *

'The play was a great success,' Oscar Wilde once said of a West End production, 'but the audience was a disaster.'

* * *

An elderly lady watching a performance of Shakespeare's *King Lear* barely allowed the curtain to swish into place after the final act before she turned to her husband and commented loudly, 'Rather an unpleasant family, those Lears.'

*   *   *

Glenda Jackson made a valiant attempt to continue performances of *The Great and the Small*, despite early warning signs from the audience. At the play's opening in Richmond, theatregoers thoughtfully waited until the interval before disappearing off home, whilst in Leeds no one turned up at all. This, however, was better than in Manchester, where the audience that did put in an appearance stormed out noisily with booing and shouts of 'rubbish'. There can be nothing more off-putting for an actor than disturbance from the audience. During one performance of *The Tempest* at the Barbican Theatre, RSC actor John Wood stopped in mid-speech to reproach a member of the audience who was desperately spluttering into a handkerchief. Having done this, Wood continued to deliver his speech. Later, the comic figure Trincolo made his entrance, clearing his throat as he did so. Remembering what had just occurred, he slapped his hand over his mouth and groaned.

*   *   *

Tired of audiences who snorted, talked, coughed or ate during his performances, cellist Julian Lloyd Webber started a 'Ssh' campaign with a cough sweet manufacturer. Pictures of the star with his finger to his mouth were to be distributed in the hope that audiences might take note. Julian claimed that the two greatest offenders were bleeping digital watches and hearing aids which make a loud screaming noise. Once, whilst he was halfway through a performance of Chopin's 'Sonata in B flat', a hearing aid went off on the note A. Julian said, 'It was a terrible cacophany and I stopped and said, "Does anybody know where that noise is coming from?" The audience looked most embarrassed and shuffled about uncomfortably.'

* * *

A stage recreation of the steam age left some theatregoers crying, when a stove which was supposed to provide the fumes of a train went mad. Actors in the play at the Norbury Theatre in Bromsgrove sat around the stove in the life-like station waiting-room. But when the curtain was raised thick fumes started to waft into the audience, leaving them coughing and spluttering and with tears streaming down their faces. The stove was removed.

Theatregoer Martie Wernz followed her favourite play to the letter and ended up being banned from the theatre. It all started when Martie, a student from Indiana, saved up £750 to travel to see her heroine, Lauren Bacall, in the musical *Applause* at Her Majesty's Theatre in London. The show is about a girl who manages to sneak into a star's dressing-room, then into her life and finally becomes bigger than the star herself. Martie seemed to be doing just that. Having seen the show a total of 46 times, Martie had tried slipping backstage to see Miss Bacall. In the end, however, it was her rapturous applause which led her to being banned from her usual front row seat. Fellow members of the audience complained about her. The theatre spokesman explained, 'She was just too enthusiastic … she seemed to be star-struck, almost living the story of the musical.' Martie learned of her barring from the front row when she went to buy her 47th ticket and an official explained that she could only have a seat in the stalls. He added, 'But when I told her of the complaint she left the theatre looking very sad.'

* * *

In 1762, David Garrick, the actor-manager of the Drury Lane Theatre, resolved to put an end to the practice of charging only half-price for admission once five-part plays had reached the third act. There was enormous resentment over the tradition being terminated, and the public made their feelings known. One Thaddeus Fitzpatrick led a revolt by getting up mid-performance, insulting the management and demanding the restoration of the public's rights. When Garrick tried to remonstrate with him from the stage, the audience not only shouted him down, but wrecked the entire theatre, tearing out the seats.

In bygone times it was common for audiences to show their displeasure at a bad performance by hissing, spitting, and throwing objects – often rotten fruit and vegetables – at the hapless actors. Samuel Pepys' diary for the 26 January 1660 runs: 'I saw *The Lost Lady* which now do please me better than before; and here our sitting behind in a dark place, a lady spit backward upon me by mistake, not seeing me, but after seeing her to be a very pretty lady, I was not troubled by it at all.'

* * *

The first incidence of the National Anthem being sung before a performance took place at the Drury

Theatre in 1745. The practice took off so rapidly that it became acceptable for the audience to sing it up to half a dozen times during every show. Such was the enthusiasm for patriotic caterwauling that eventually volunteer officers started to stand up mid-performance and insist that the show be halted until the audience had sung at least a couple of verses of 'God Save The King'.

*   *   *

Wendy Roe was so good as the baddie in a Sheffield production of *Pinocchio* that the audience attacked her. In true panto tradition, 17-year-old Wendy dressed up in a cat costume and inspired lots of hissing and booing from her young spectators. However, when she ran through the aisles, the kids set upon her. One child tripped her up as she ran past, and then a group of 5- to 8-year-olds held her down, so that the panto policeman could arrest her. Wendy had to be rescued by fellow actors, who jumped from the stage and pulled her from a veritable scrum. Limping back to the stage with cuts and bruises – and minus her cat's tail – Wendy felt lucky to have escaped with her life. She admitted later than she couldn't believe what had happened adding, 'Next year I want to be a goodie.' Just to be on the safe side, the director had Wendy's runaround scene dropped from the play.

*　　*　　*

A production of Edward Bond's *Lear* at the Barbican came with a health warning for timid theatregoers. Patrons were advised that some of the scenes in the play might be found disturbing; these unspeakable acts included women being kicked and bayoneted to death, and tortures involving knitting needles. In fact, some scenes were so revolting that on one night 2 people were sick and another 20 left the play before the end. In a transparent attempt to play the thing down, the Royal Shakespeare Company retorted that these people had left early to 'catch the last bus home'.

*　　*　　*

Elizabeth Scott, a 66-year-old widow, loved seaside shows so much that she sat through the entire run of a three-month show at Morecambe, Lancashire. Elizabeth could be seen six nights a week in the same front row seat. She kept coming year after year until the tradition seemed to have reached its natural end, when she took a job as a nanny in New York. To make matters worse, she had a heart attack and couldn't make the trip to

Morecambe even for a few performances. So the show's company rang up their Number One fan and gave her a special performance down a transatlantic telephone line. The star of the show, Ronnie Coyles, gathered the cast together and treated Elizabeth to the show's highlights, which included a rendition of 'Beautiful Dreamer' by soprano Karen Simmons. Over in Manhattan, Elizabeth was overjoyed. 'It was just what the doctor ordered – a real seaside tonic. At £14.31 for the call it was almost as cheap as a Broadway ticket – and much more enjoyable. Afterwards I promised, God willing, that I'd be back in the same seat at their show next year.'

*   *   *

The great Rex Harrison once stalked off stage in the middle of a performance of *Bell, Book and Candle* and refused to return until a baby had been removed from the audience.

*   *   *

Tom Courtenay, taking the lead role in *Billy Liar*, was also disturbed by a noisy audience. In fact, during one scene in which he was on the stage alone, he stepped into the footlights and remonstrated with them. 'Please be quiet,' he said. 'I can't go on if you make all this noise.'

*   *   *

Charles Laughton had persevered despite interruptions by a heckler throughout his performance in *The Party*. Finally he lost it and, turning to the audience, said, 'I think we'd better drop the curtain until this gentleman is removed.' Spike Milligan used the same threat during his performance of *Son of Oblomov*, with different results. For, on announcing that unless the heckler was silent the curtain would be brought down, the heckler retorted, 'You wouldn't dare.' True to his word, Milligan left the stage and the curtain swished into place.

*   *   *

A tender moment between Tony and Maria in the passionate musical *West Side Story*, was destroyed when a man from the audience jumped up and screamed, 'Stop the show! My wife should be singing that song.' The audience at the Grand Theatre in Swansea turned to look at the gentleman ranting in the upper circle. After refusing to keep quiet, he had to be dragged from the hall and into a side bar, where several lights were smashed. The man was finally taken away for questioning, allowing Tony and Maria to continue with their rendition of 'Tonight'. Peter Jay-Scott, the manager of the touring theatre company, explained that many women had auditioned for the prestigious role of Maria, adding, 'His wife could have been one of them.'

* * *

The Vermuyden players from Doncaster were preparing for a packed first night after slavish weeks of rehearsals. But when the curtain went up on the amateur dramatic production they were faced with 299 empty seats and a lone man. 63-year-old Arthur Hallam was offered his money back and asked to leave. But Arthur was adamant. He'd paid his 25p to see the show and he wanted his money's worth. So the show went on. Two hours later, after sitting through the three one-act comedies, Arthur commented, 'They were pretty good for a first night. I felt a bit alone but I thought it was only right that I see the show.' As a result, the company contemplated changing their name, because they thought it might be a bit off-putting. However, things looked decidedly better on the second night, when an audience of 47 turned up ... until it was discovered that 20 of these were members of a scout troop run by the producer.

* * *

One American theatregoer couldn't stand his favourite poet being criticised on stage, so he started arguing with the actors. The play, *The Barretts of Wimpole Street* was showing at the Lyric, London in 1965, and the Yank with the Robert Browning obsession was sitting in the royal box. When one of the characters voiced criticism about the play, which Browning, played by another actor, had written, the theatregoer jumped out of his expensive seat, shouting 'Nonsense'. The American continued his support for the actor playing Browning for a full 20 minutes, while the cast tried to continue with the play. 'It's a rotten play,' said the actor, continuing with the script. 'It's a good play,' interjected the American, adding at the top of his voice, 'and he's a good painter, too.' Finally, one of the theatre staff had to have a quiet word with the heated gentleman. Later, unable to stand his poetic mentor receiving a roasting, albeit on stage, the American left.

* * *

Actor David Goderson was truly marooned when not a single soul turned up to see his one-man play, fittingly entitled *The Castaway*. An actor through and through, however, David gave the performance of his life to 225 vacant seats and two usherettes resting their feet in the front row. David, who had also written the play, was disappointed at the response, since he had been on TV and radio to publicise it. The play, based on the life of the reclusive poet William Cowper, obviously failed to engage public interest, leaving David to confess, 'I felt a bit of a castaway on the stage with no audience. During the play I am supposed to age from 26 to 65 and I nearly did.' He added as a small consolation, 'The usherettes enjoyed it. They clapped at the end.'

*   *   *

The director of one new play strode confidently on to the stage on opening night to be faced with a horror of horrors. There on the front row was showman Jack Hylton – fast asleep. This was the bad omen that every actor dreads. The cast tried their utmost to arouse Hylton from his slumber, but even when the star of the show kicked a TV set and smoke filled the stage, Jack continued to sleep peacefully.

*   *   *

Noel Coward once displayed his feelings about a

lack-lustre audience on an opening night by executing a low bow – in the opposite direction.

* * *

The five members of The Theatre of Mistakes encouraged audience participation during their performances in the Serpentine Gallery, London. However, one show, based on their interpretation of an eighteenth-century Venetian painter, caused a little more participation than they were banking on. One member of the audience approached an actress and aimed a punch at her. After that, there was artistic mayhem, in which the actors eventually had physically to stop the audience from turning on one another. One actor, Anthony Howell, said the scene had been scandalous. He described the man responsible for the fisticuffs as 'an upper-class lout who had obviously had too much to drink'. Neither did Howell know what the actress had done to offend the man. At the moment of the attempted attack she had been in the middle of singing 'Give My Regards to Broadway'.

* * *

In 1989, leading businessmen received lessons on the etiquette of going to the theatre. Advice included not hogging the bar and wearing appropriate dress. For example, if the rest of the audience was wearing informal clothes, the businessmen were advised to follow suit and not to go togged up in evening dress. These guidelines came from the Association of Business Sponsorship of the Arts, after complaints from audience members that the invitees of sponsors often didn't know the correct way to behave at performances. One theatre critic in the *Guardian* reported that he was prevented from enjoying a production of *Hamlet* because the invitees of Ladbrokes, the play's sponsors, insisted on talking throughout; whether they had been laying bets on the outcome of Hamlet's 'To be or not to be' dilemma was unclear. Concern was also growing over the first night parties which sponsors threw for the leading actors. The guidelines pointed out that after a performance an actor might wish to spend time with friends or simply resting.

* * *

In 1989, a play which was billed as 'the strangest theatrical event of the decade' opened in London. To be pedantic, *You: The City* wasn't really a play because the audience were as important as the actors. The stage was roughly located on and around the streets of the East End, and the only props required were umbrellas, in case of rain.

The 'theatregoers' would be sent off on their own through a maze of streets, where they would be met by the actors at designated points. The official players would be masquerading as taxi drivers, spies, or ranting members of the public. Each client would be subjected to 10 minutes of lecturing and questioning before being passed on to the next actor. The theatregoers did not meet each other until they all converged in the pub at the end of the evening. This form of entertainment was first undertaken in New York, where it induced one critic to report: 'You might well believe you have been plugged into a nightmare.' Fiona Templeton, the woman responsible for writing the event and bringing it to the streets of London, advised clients to bring 'comfortable shoes and an open mind'.

5

This One Will Run and Run . . . The Price of Fame

A jobless actor who was £16,000 in debt held up a cashier in the Trustee Savings Bank in Avon by threatening her with a banana. The actor, aged 25, got away with £4,000 because the cashier thought that the piece of fruit in his pocket was a gun. However, the actor later confessed to the crime and was subsequently jailed for two years.

* * *

One RSC actor, Paul Greenwood, playing in *The Happiest Days of Your Life*, suffered the ultimate embarrassment of forgetting his lines not once, but twice. One critic remarked that Mr Greenwood had dried up so often that his requests for help from the prompter almost became part of the script. Another, seemingly uninspired by the script, commented that it was not surprising that Mr Greenwood would wish to forget it. A third critic made reference to the Barbican's prompting service, which he likened to the announcement system at Victoria Station – loud and unintelligible. When Mr Greenwood finally managed a performance without prompting, his relieved smile said it all.

* * *

Charlie Chaplin once entered a Charlie Chaplin lookalike competition in Monaco... he came third.

* * *

Norman Wisdom once stayed at a bed and breakfast digs in Barrow-In-Furness. Feeling under the bed in the dark for a chamber-pot he felt something else, and struck a match – to find a dead body! Norman went to the police who discovered that the previous evening the landlady's husband had died and she had put the body under the bed!

* * *

The lead role in Shakespeare's *Hamlet* seems to have a profound effect on any actor who undertakes it. Daniel Day Lewis had to withdraw from the role at the National Theatre due to nervous exhaustion. Day Lewis, having just told Horatio that 'there are more things in heaven and earth than are dreamt of in your philosophy' promptly collapsed. Kenneth Branagh described the fear which had overtaken him whilst playing the Danish prince: 'The stomach-wrenching feeling that overtakes one as the first soliloquy begins is truly terrifying.' Similarly, Sir Laurence Olivier, playing the role at the National Theatre in 1964, admitted to feelings of terror. Anxious in case he forgot all his lines, Olivier took to spending his lunch hours practising in secret with his stage manager. He insisted that, instead of just rehearsing his own lines, she read the entire play with him. Added to this, he couldn't stand being left alone on stage during his soliloquies and asked Frank Finlay to stay in the wings where he could see him. Later, whilst playing the role of Shylock in the Bard's *Merchant of Venice*, Olivier was once again visited by the terrors. He implored his fellow actors not to look him directly in the eyes on the first night, for fear that he would forget his lines. However, the sense of fear did not abate, and a short time before curtain up, Larry was threatening to hop aboard the first bus that stopped

outside the Old Vic. Luckily, he went on stage –
and gave one of his finest performances.

* * *

Alma Cogan found herself flat on her back during
a Savoy charity show in the presence of Princess
Margaret. Nevertheless, she gamely carried on
singing, sitting on her bruises.

* * *

Actor Tom Selleck, of *Three Men and a Baby* fame,
started off his film career by appearing in a blue
movie called *Daughters of Satan*. His demanding
role consisted of chasing a voluptuous actress
who was wearing a transparent top. Later Tom
moved on to better things by starring in the film
Coma – as a man suffering from one.

* * *

Meg Ryan, star of *When Harry Met Sally*, had her
first major role in an American TV soap called *As
The World Turns*. Meg said of her part, 'In two years
on that show I was kidnapped, abused, raped and
impregnated.' No doubt having had enough
drama to last a lifetime, Meg chose a more sedate
role in the horror-movie *Amityville* III.

*　　*　　*

Cheers star Ted Danson started his successful career by impersonating a lemon chiffon pie box in a TV ad. He then made a name for himself by advertising Aramis aftershave, before getting a part in the TV soap *The Doctors*.

*　　*　　*

Sean Connery had an inauspicious start in the acting business – he took part in a Mr Universe competition in Edinburgh. This led him to a stage part in the musical *South Pacific*. The man who was to become James Bond could be seen in the chorus, belting out 'There Is Nothing Like a Dame' . . . Connery has not been known to sing in public since.

*　　*　　*

The Intimate Revue at the Duchess Theatre, London was an ambitious little show. It involved so many scene changes, some of which took 20 minutes, that the directors had to scrap 7 of them in order for the finale to take place before midnight.

*　　*　　*

The West End musical *South Pacific* was renowned for its fantastic water displays, but the audience at the Prince of Wales Theatre was not prepared for these to be participatory affairs. Just after actress Jenny Michelmore had sung 'I'm Going to Wash that Man Right Out of My Hair', a safety curtain cut through a water pipe. Hundreds of gallons of water gushed out over the stage, orchestra pit and auditorium. Many instruments in the pit were ruined, leaving all the show's musicians to find replacements. Frantic staff had to dry off and repaint the sumptuous set in order to go ahead with the show the next day. Theatregoers who had been subjected to a soaking were offered tickets for future performances. A theatre spokesman said that although the audience had been disappointed to miss the entire show they had been understanding, with the exception of the inevitable American who had threatened to contact his lawyer.

* * *

In 1991, *Sale of the Century*'s Nicholas Parsons was host to an audience of just four. But following one of the oldest rules of showbusiness, namely that the show must go on, Parsons gamely went ahead with his 90-minute performance. Parsons, then 63, had been paid £750 by the Charles Cryer

Theatre in Surrey to do his one-man one-off show. The crowd of four sat in the middle of the theatre when Parsons came on stage. After cracking a few jokes about it, Parsons continued with his act. At the end of his performance he turned to his small but loyal audience and said, 'I think we all deserve a drink now.'

*   *   *

As Phil Donaghy fell to the floor in his dramatic death scene, the audience applauded wildly. What they didn't know was that the replica gun used to send Phil to meet his maker had misfired, showering him with gunpowder. The result was agony as he took the blast right in the face, but Phil carried on until the last curtain call had been taken at the Everyman Theatre in Liverpool. The audience remained in the dark about the whole incident. The only giveaway was when Phil came on stage the next day with a patch over one eye.

*   *   *

Actors in one open-air production in St Neots, Cambridgeshire found that a night on stage was rather chilly, especially in their flimsy Grecian costumes. In an attempt to combat the problem they took to wearing highly un-classical gym shorts under their tunics to keep the wind out.

*　　*　　*

A television salesman won £2,000 under a Government enterprise allowance scheme to become a travelling showman. Keith Willmott, 33, of Somerset boasted talents for singing, mind-reading and escapology.

*　　*　　*

Leslie Crowther spent a night in Bradford at a boarding house which had an outside lavatory. During the middle of the night Crowther had to spend a penny, so he set off down the garden path towards the outhouse. As he made his way in the dark, a casement window opened and his land-lady popped her head out. 'Mr Crowther!' she called. 'Are you going to the lavatory?' 'Yes,' he whispered. 'Well,' she continued, 'don't go in that one, luv. It's next door's and we're not speaking!'

*　　*　　*

Such is Peter Elliott's expertise at imitating apes that he landed himself a role of Silverbeard, the lead monkey in the film *Greystoke*. Peter has also tutored almost 1,000 people to behave like apes. His knowledge of the behaviour of our closest cousins has been hard-won. As well as successfully merging and living with a chimp colony, Peter also visits zoos regularly to refresh his ape-apeing skills. On three occasions he has been mauled and he lost the use of his little finger after becoming engaged in a debate with some chimps. Yet Peter has mastered the art of monkeying around to such an extent that Los Angeles police once took pot-shots at him whilst he was sitting in a tree, believing him to be a chimp. On the other hand, being capable of imitating an ape has its benefits. Peter recalls an incident in a tube station when a man was hassling him. He added, 'I just gave him a pant hoot, all teeth bared, and he backed off pretty sharpish. The interesting thing was that everyone stared at the man for being the culprit and left me alone.' Peter's other acting accomplishments include having played Quasimodo and a bacteria germ for a toothpaste advert.

*   *   *

The theatre's greatest rival is the television. One theatre manager blamed lack of audiences on the fact that *Coronation Street*'s Ken and Deirdre were having so many emotional bust-ups. Derek

Coleman, manager of the Pomegranate Theatre in Chesterfield gave this explanation when there was only one booking in his 600-seat theatre on the day he started work. He said forlornly, 'I know that the pubs were empty too.' The critic of the local paper noticed the lack of public response to the production of *Dancing Dan*. He described the show as, 'Excellent' with 'virtuoso performances' and the audience as 'a figment of the imagination'.

* * *

The seven players of the Littlehampton Theatre Club were staging a production of *A Little Bit of Love Besides*, but besides one man in the audience, the 75-seat theatre was on the empty side. In fact, the sole gentleman sitting in the middle of the front row was treated to a private performance. As the curtain fell, the token theatregoer clapped politely, then made a quick exit.

* * *

Bank manager Buster Merryfield had dreamed all his life of forsaking the boredom of the financial world for the precarious life of an actor. So at the age of 57, when most people are thinking of giving it all up, Buster applied for a job at every theatre within striking distance. He received one reply, which offered him the position of assistant stage manager – responsibilities to include emptying the ashtrays. Undeterred, Buster accepted, and for the next six years he enjoyed consistent work, including a role in Anglia TV's *Shroud For A Nightingale*. 'I am always cast as a professional man,' he commented, 'either a bishop or a doctor – but not a bank manager as yet.'

*   *   *

A report by the Health Education Authority came to the conclusion that some actors would have to start smoking if they wanted to work. This glum news came after a survey of almost 100 actors who admitted that they had had to smoke to get parts in plays and films. The actors said that after having been asked to do it in a production, they tended to start, or take it up again. The lecturer responsible for the survey claimed, 'Acting is probably the only profession where an ability and willingness to smoke is almost a prerequisite of the job.' He continued, 'It is no good arguing with the author or director that smoking is not necessary, because often the answer is, "We'll get someone else." ' Another aspect to bear in mind, according to the researcher, was that while you may only see an actor smoke half a cigarette in a particular scene, he may have had to do exactly the same thing through 30 retakes or rehearsals.

*   *   *

Police in Hartlepool engaged actors to help them simulate a gas leak emergency at a chemical plant; they soon wished they hadn't, reported *Police* magazine in August 1993. In his official memo on the incident, an Inspector Turnbull reported, 'It didn't start well. The actors pretending to be casualty victims arrived three hours late and there was some sort of argument about catering and who would get "star billing" ' Things got worse, the Inspector went on. One thespian had a severe asthma attack on a high gantry, three others complained of hypothermia and the exercise was aborted. 'God alone knows what will happen if there ever really is a leak at the plant,' the Inspector concluded. 'Its the last time I work with actors.'